SAI BABA
An Incarnation

An Incarnation

Though the sky is beset with stars
    but the moon has a unique identity...
As though showing us the
    right path, even in darkness...
Many near, dear ones walk with
    us on this path of life,
Who entangle our life in a karmic cycle
    and become reasons for the
    sway of karmas in our life...
They become the reasons for
    filling our life with religion,
Maya etc., and always stay
    near and around us...
But to show us the path of devotion
    to stabilise the feet that are
wavering on the vagrant base of Maya,
    and to show us the path of salvation
to walk on this path with us...
    To merge us into our own self
it seems as though the moon
    itself has come to the earth...
To give the Godly touch,
    joy of the soul to
We Humans, lost in a web of Maya,
    God Himself incarnates on this
earth for our benefit
    By binding the Godly self

to the parameters of a body
An Incarnation is born.
In every Yuga, again and again many a times.
He appears solely for our benefit.
By binding Himself to the enactments, bondages of bodily deeds.
He takes different names and forms
at times Rama or Krishna
and in this Kalyug as Sai.
The incarnation any, the name may vary but the aim is one— Human Upliftment
Our elation from the darkness of Maya to the light of the Lord.
Through their leelas they give us their silent deep messages.
The messages that have the seed of Human existence hidden in them.
The messages in which the Lord Himself is seated.
The messages that we have to adorn,
understand, gather and assimilate to the greatest depths.
As it's here that you will 'see' the Lord.
It's here that the Lord's true identity will shine.
It's here that the Lord will introduce you to your true self.
God will merge you into His own self through this incarnated form.
Even while in human form,
God will hold your hand (as the incarnated form) and merge you in His true identity (the divine self).
He will accept and merge you in
His Loving, Godly, Divine self.
He will carry you beyond this worldly ocean
And make you reach the true mission of human life.
—Merging in the Lord

So be it! Om Sai Ram!

Shri Ganeshaya Namah

Hari Om Tat Sat Jai Guru Datta

Om Sai Ram!

SAI BABA
An Incarnation

Bela Sharma

STERLING PAPERBACKS
An imprint of
Sterling Publishers (P) Ltd.
Regd. Office: A-59, Okhla Industrial Area, Phase-II,
New Delhi-110020. CIN: U22110PB1964PTC002569
Tel: 26387070, 26386209; Fax: 91-11-26383788
E-mail: mail@sterlingpublishers.com
www.sterlingpublishers.com

Sai Baba: An Incarnation
© 2014, Bela Sharma
ISBN 978 81 207 8833 6

All rights are reserved.
No part of this publication may be reproduced, stored in a retrieval system or transmitted, in any form or by any means, mechanical, photocopying, recording or otherwise, without prior written permission of the author.

Printed in India

Printed and Published by Sterling Publishers Pvt. Ltd., New Delhi-110020.

Dedicated at the Lotus feet of our friend, mother, father, beloved, our every thing—Lord 'Sai Baba'—a saintly incarnation of the Lord. We surrender our all to him.

For My Husband

The grace of the Godly incarnation, Sai Baba that is enveloped in this book is a humble gift of this body and soul to my husband, Vinod Sharma as it is my husband who always showed me the path of honesty, simplicity and goodness, to move closer to the Lord Almighty. By his honest and genuine deeds he showed me practically that even in this Kalyug by leading a life fully paved for other's enhancement fills us with complete inner satisfaction. This goodness, honesty and service to humanity, fills us with a sense of satiation that leads us to Sai and shows us the path of His Divine home—the path of salvation. Thank you Lord Sai that you gave me your loving companionship as my husband.

Preface

Since time immemorial the very existence of humans on earth is based on the threshold of faith and it's this faith that paves our path in life till we cross the ocean of mundane existence. Each one has his or her own faith, which varies from one being to another. Some worship God in a particular form, some connect to the Lord within and some others see God in their Karmas. We may worship God in any way, call Him by any name, admire Him in any form but the aim of all is the same—self-realisation, merging of the self into the selfless or the divine, illuminous self within, it revealing itself to us.

Since we humans dwell in a form, hence it is easier for us to worship God in a form. We do believe in the omnipresence of God but being ourselves bound to a form we are not able to fully understand and assimilate the formless nature of God. To play on the strings of devotion within us, to remove the veil of Maya engulfing us, to introduce us to our own true self, to show us a glimpse of the Lord Almighty, to use this decaying body as a means to reach the immortal, Lord Himself incarnates on this planet earth, as Ram, Krishna or Sai. Through His varied *leelas* in each incarnation the *Leeladhar* explains to each one of us; practically shows us through His bodily deeds that how we mortals can attain the Lord even while dwelling in the bondages of a body, how we can reach the omnipotent, formless, our true self through the medium of this body, how we have to attain that true self and ultimately lose ourselves in the identity of the Lord.

Lord incarnated in this *Kalyug* as a saint—Sai. Sai meaning the Lord God Himself, making Shirdi His Karma Bhoomi and all His life He lived in a dilapidated mosque. He, through His apparent deeds taught us how to live a simple, satisfactory spiritual life, how to live a satiated life as it's a gift of God to us. While executing our duties with full dedication and honesty we must always keep chanting the Lord's name. Dedicating all our deeds, our life at His Lotus feet, we should have complete faith in His name and His grace.

While in Shirdi, Baba showed innumerable leelas, the deeper and true meaning of some were revealed there and then but some were and are still being unveiled with the passage of time. The deeper and true meanings hidden behind each leela have not been fully understood by anyone and it's difficult that anyone can unveil so many different messages to their true depth. Yet when His grace is showered then some precious jewels do surface from that deep ocean— Sai.

The so called bodily functions, deeds, big and small experiences showered on His devotees are called His leelas. His leelas are His silent language, oozing ambrosia, which are understood to the deepest core by very few. We are bound to His Lotus feet mostly due to the miracles, which were performed bodily to ignite faith in us, we were and are unable to gather the deeper meaning of the miracles performed and the true meaning remained behind the veils. This silent truth, the divine depth of Baba's incarnation, sometimes surfaced as a result of His grace. This hidden truth, the divine depth Sai, which was not understood by us, in His miracles or words, kept saying something in its silent, yet deep voice. This effort is an attempt to put to light, unveil, gather and understand these silent yet deep messages of Baba. This is purely a shower of Sai's 'grace'. This mortal coil, the thoughts, this name are merely means, rest all is the Lord's grace, the magnificent doing of the leeladhar, Sai who is the doer of all.

Preface

Our past, present and future, all have been paved by our Sai. So keep doing your duty with whatever means and situations He has created for us—do not repent for the past instead learn from the errors of the past, do not waste your today as it will soon be past and do not worry for your future as it will merely retard your pace today and worry will make you weaker—physically and mentally. Take all that comes your way as the command of the Lord, live your life according to the needs and demands of your today, leaving all in the hands of the Lord. Surrender all at His Lotus feet—your ego, happiness—sorrow. Love the Lord, worship Him, meditate on Him and direct the mission of your life to achieve Him. Then see how He accepts you, how He makes your body and thoughts a means to spread His name, how He slowly unfurls His true self to you; even that which is still left hidden in veils is granted to you by His grace, turning your life towards liberation, hence fructifying this human life.

This book has been accomplished by this mortal body, but the thoughts enclosed here are offshoots that surfaced while chanting His name. Truly Sai, the Lord God alone who fully and wholly controls this body and mind. Thank you Sai for making me a means for your tasks. Thank you Baba for granting the boon of your name to this tool of yours, hence, making this life worthwhile. Some of the text in this book has been published in the *Sai Leela* Magazine (Shirdi) in hindi.

Bela Sharma
A-3/154 Janak Puri
New Delhi-110058
Email: belasharma@rediffmail.com
Ph: 9868867940/011-25521167

Contents

	For My Husband	viii
	Preface	ix
1.	Saints—The Living Form of God	1
2.	Saints—the Connecting Force between God and a Devotee	6
3.	Immortal Incarnation	12
4.	The 'Lotus Feet' of the Lord	21
5.	Magnanimity of God's Name	31
6.	God—An Experience	36
7.	The Significance of Guru *Sthaan*	39
8.	Three Steps in the Dwarkamaayi and the Samadhi Mandir	45
9.	Baba's resting in the Dwarkamaayi and the Chavadi	54
10.	Why did Baba (or other Saints) Smoke the Chillum	67
11.	True Significance of Butter	71
12.	Shyam Kund, Radha Kund	79
13.	Solar Eclipse	85
14.	Baba's Brick	90
15.	Sai Maa in Dwarkamaayi	97
16.	Khandoba Temple	104
17.	Nanda Deep	107
18.	Amni's One Rupee	111

19. True Richness or Lordship is Hidden in *Fakiri*   116
20. Samadhi Mandir (Form of Lakshmi–Narayan)   121
21. Touch of the Samadhi, Joy of the Pothi
    (*Sai Sat Charita*) and Udi, Solution to all
    Problems   127
22. Why did Baba Adorn the Kafni?   140
23. I was, I am, I always will be...   148

1

Saints — The Living Form of God

Saints are living forms of the Lord. They take a form to connect this body to the soul, hence introducing this body to the soul within. The body and the soul are linked with each other as a flower to its fragrance, as the light with the sun or as wetness with water. Yet to be able to understand this fact, that this body is the means to reach the soul within, we keep spinning in the cycle of birth and rebirth. A saint is that link who holds the hand of the body, introduces it to its true self — the soul that is dwelling inside us, the soul that is a part of the supersoul. Some people regard saints as messengers of God, truly they are the Lord God Himself who has incarnated on this earth.

We mortals are usually unable to assimilate the oneness of a Saint and God, and keep taking saints as ordinary living beings who have come on this earth like us ordinary beings adorning a mortal coil. Actually there is no difference between a Saint and the Lord. The Lord Himself appears as a Saint on this earth for the upliftment and the enhancement of this entire creation. Lord Krishna too has said that Saints are His own living forms, His representatives. *Sai Sat Charita* also states that we bathe in sacred rivers for submerging our misdeeds or negative Karmas in them but these sacred rivers are ever eager to get a kiss of the pious feet of the Saints.

Human nature is based on doubt; hence, it is difficult to erect the flag of faith when such doubt exists. Human beings always and mostly engulf themselves in the parameters of me or mine, good or bad deeds. We go to religious places for the fulfilment of our desires but it's only a rare one amongst us who loses himself in the Love of the Lord and that too by His grace only. We foolish, unripe beings are unable to understand the real God and are mostly lost in our own doubts. Surrender and faith is tougher than proofs and arguments for us obstinate mortals. Our entire lifetime is spent in proving our own point according to our own individual thoughts. This is the gift that has been assigned to the fading face of humanity in this Kalyug.

To generate faith in the ever-doubting being, to introduce him to His own true self, the Lord incarnated on this earth in the form of a Saint. But this doubting human, instead of knowing and recognising the Lord who advented as a saint, always keeps doubting and so he is unable to have full faith in a saint who outwardly looks and appears as himself—an ordinary human. He feels that the saint is not different from him. He sees the outer form and assumes it to be the same as his own, and the inner soul that they both carry seems no different to him. Even now if we do not understand the true identity of a Saint, then there is little hope for us. It's time we recognised and understood the true identity, the omnipresence, the divine self, that is, the Lord God Himself.

After all what is the difference between a human being and the extraordinary saint, who has adorned a simple mortal coil?

The Lord's identity as a soul is an integral part of each being and as they say that the soul is very small but at the same time it is very large too, that is, it is the smallest and yet the largest. It's being in its smallest form, that is, the soul is portrayed in us humans. A very small speck of the supersoul, as our soul surfaces in an ordinary human being, which guides us to pave the path of salvation for our own selves, from within ourselves. On the other hand we can experience and understand the largeness of this soul in a Saint. Humans only carry a speck of the soul while a saint engulfs the entire universe, as the Lord Himself has incarnated on the earth. For example, a speck of rice in a container is like the the soul in us mortals, and to gather the entire rice production of this earth in a container depicts the vastness of the supersoul, a Saint.

Let us now turn towards the deeds performed by us. All actions performed by us generate our *Karmic* cycle, that is, a cycle or flow of deeds and their fruits. These deeds are the cause of all joy—sorry, elation, depression, etc., in our life. Our deeds are good or bad, right or wrong and it's these deeds that entangle us in a cycle of birth and rebirth or they push us closer to our true mission in life, that is, liberation. On the other hand, the bodily deeds performed by a saint are not Karmas though they may look like ordinary deeds only. These deeds are termed as leelas that are performed by the saint. We will try to understand the difference between Karmas and leelas, by His grace. We perform Karmas for our own elation, for our own upliftment so that we can reach closer to the soul within by making this body a means for the same. But we mortals keep falling in the pit of Maya, by generating our own digression. On the other hand, the leelas performed by an incarnation of God, the apparent deeds performed by the Lord in the form of a saint, are actually actions performed for the upliftment of all. Leelas performed by a saint are pregnant with the hidden, deeper messages of God, which we either understand spontaneously or its true meaning unfurls itself slowly with the flow of time. The fact is that each leela positively carries a deep message for us, that is, every leela pushes us in one way or another towards humanity and goodness; towards the Lord or towards our own progress.

Further, we are so influenced by Maya, that our attachment to this body, the dark engulfment of Maya, the horrifying yet delusive and soothing presence of the five elements of nature in the body, do not let us reach our true identity—the form of the Lord inside us, that is, the soul. The artificial identity of the body overpowers the true identity of the soul. So even while being aware of our true mission we keep falling into the deep darkness of greed, jealousy, hatred. As a result we keep suffering in the lower life forms, we digress or regress. On the other hand, saints are the living forms of the Lord Himself, their body being a mere outward veil, a means. The truth, the basis of all, and the Lord Himself surfaces in the form of a Saint by totally and fully crossing the threshold of the body. This body, a slave of duality, makes a futile effort to gather and imbibe the Divinity inherent in a Saint. The Divine glory or illuminative light reveals itself over and over again in a saint because the body is unable to hide or conceal this omnipotent, indivisible divine light of the Lord. An ordinary human coil is like an iron door that blocks the light fully from being revealed while the mortal coil adorned by a saint is like a glass door that cannot hinder the light within from spreading all over even in closed doors such as inside the body.

We humans have been given this mortal coil as a means to reach our basic within, but the limited parameters of our body, the selfish norms of I and mine, and the six enemies—anger, greed, lust, jealousy, ego, and temptation—that generate sorrow and create hurdles in our lives, keep pushing us away from the path of elation towards digression. On the other hand, the mortal coil adorned by a Saint is a mere outward covering that keeps making futile efforts to cover and conceal the divinity within. This Divinity keeps overpowering the smallness and hollowness of the mortal body to reveal its light over and over again. We mortals understand this Godly, God's divine living form, along with the deeds performed by the saints, as miracles. This divinity conveys to us how we have to merge our Karmas into leelas even while dwelling within the parameters of our mortal body. We have to understand that this body is not the end but a medium to reach the end which is the speck of the Lord within us, that is, the soul. This can be achieved by binding all the forms of the Lord, that is, all souls, by one thread and hence becoming the Lord Himself, and in the process understand our true identity, be one with His omnipresent identity, embrace His divine self and merge our identity in Him and attain salvation. While dwelling in this human coil we have to hold the hand of a Saint, through Him, attain the unending form of the Lord and merge into the same. We have to give the soul its true identity that has been changing innumerable forms of many lives. We have to ultimately merge into peace (God) and rest in the same for ages to come. We can attain the true mission of our life by losing ourselves in the embrace of peace, that is, God.

All leelas performed by a saint are basically for our benefit as each leela has God's unknown facts hidden within it. Each leela conveys to us the unknown feel of the Divinity. God Himself rests in each leela, each leela reveals the unseen depths to us. To unveil these deeper meanings conveyed by the Lord, Baba's grace shines on us. Try to know and understand the silent language of the Lord. That silent language that Baba is revealing to us even today, as always. It's only with His Divine grace, His orders that these silent words have been woven. His blessings have accomplished this task by weaving a garland of the deeper meanings of His leelas and the same has been offered at His Lotus feet.

Shri Sai Leela (Shirdi), May–June 2010

2

Saints — the Connecting Force between God and a Devotee

Though opposite in nature yet the soul and the body have been very closely bound together, where one is a medium for the liberation of the other, because it is the body that is the medium to liberate the soul. Actually we all sway in innumerable opposites, all our life. The identity of life surfaces on the unification of the body and the soul. The two basic ends of life are also opposites, that is, life and death, and within these two opposites we face many opposed and extreme situations, we struggle through them, such as happiness–sorrow, light–darkness, elation–digression, etc., unaccountable number of times.

Why did God create this body to be a means for the liberation of the soul within? An attempt is made to explain the same with an example. We need utensils to cook food, a glass or bottle to drink water and beverages, a bag to carry our things or else all would be scattered. We need wires for electricity to reach our homes, a house to stay in. We need different things for different tasks. In the same way the soul too needs a means, that is, a body for paving its path leading to *Mukti* (deliverance).

It is believed that the living force, the soul, inside us is the basis of life; it is an integral and indivisible part of the Lord Almighty. This body is merely the coming together of the five elements of nature—water, air, sky, fire and earth—that merge back into nature once their life tenure is over, that is, when the basis of life, the soul, departs or leaves this body.

It has been said by learned souls that knowledge cannot be taught or gathered because the Lord's light is not going to appear from the outside as this Divine light is always present inside us as our soul. Our soul, our true divine self has been concealed from us as it is inside us, hence we are not familiar with it. Maya creates an illusion around us and we take only Maya, that is, the body to be real and the light, that is, life behind this Maya seems to be unreal. This illusion is so magnanimous that it easily enslaves us, fully sinking us in itself. The intoxication of Maya is so deep that the truth, the divine light behind this Maya seems to vanish and hence seems unreal.

We poor human beings came to this earth to gather knowledge of the self, to discover the true self within but lose ourselves to the intoxicating effect of Maya. Under the intoxication of Maya, we are happy to call ourselves knowledgeable while actually we are unable to get even the slightest feel of what is true knowledge.

We forget that we cannot gain knowledge merely by reading texts or listening to discourses, or making an attempt to prove ourselves superior to others. We merely have to remove the veil of ignorance for knowledge to shine to its fullest. We have to fully get rid of the intoxication of Maya, by regularly chanting the Lord's name so that our true identity illuminates on its own. To move towards and to reach this basic, that is, the soul within, reading religious texts and singing His glory are the means for elation.

By merely claiming that we are knowledgeable or a great personality, we are allowing Maya to triumph in the form of our ego, and in the process pushing ourselves away from the true light. It is the same as wiping a fogged windowpane from the outside by all possible means instead of from the inside where the fog of Maya is engulfing us. We foolish mortals keep to the outside, not bothering to go within. If the Lord's name chanted by you had reached these inner parameters it would have automatically removed this fog of Maya, unveiling the ever-illuminative light, our true identity, that is an integral part of us. Had we removed the veil of Maya we would have been face to face with our own selves.

Many a times we talk of the elation of the soul that is part of the supersoul, by using this coil as a medium for the same. The true identity of the Lord is with the soul, because the soul is a part of the supersoul and not this body. The body is a creation of the five elements of nature, then how can the Lord be one with this body? Can oil and water ever mix? Even if we try our best to do so, the oil will continue to float on water and will never fully blend with water. The same is with God and our body. The aim of our life is that the soul and the supersoul should be face to face one day, the soul hence losing itself to the supersoul, to search its own identity. At the same time to achieve this, the means is our body, so we have to stay within the limitations of this body, our deeds. We will have to connect this soul to the Lord but only after crossing the ups and downs of our Karmas which are basic to this body.

The Lord incarnated as a Saint to be a bridge, a link between the soul and the supersoul. Saints too dwell in a body, but basically or rather wholly to ferry the soul from the bondages of the body to the flight of the supersoul.

Briefly we can say that God created us humans to be able to recognise our own true selves but we completely entangled ourselves in a tangible web of Karmas. Instead of washing away the layer of Maya and ignorance we are constantly increasing this layer due to the ignorance and darkness of Maya. When God could no longer help this foolish mortal then He incarnated as a saint, that is, he Himself appeared in a body to introduce us to His true identity. God keeps rewarding us according to our deeds—as you sow so shall you reap. If you sow *babul* (plant with thorns), you will have to tread on thorns but if you plant dates, sweetness is bound to fill your path. It is our deeds that either put us on the path of progress or push us in the mire of digression. The Lord is fully love incarnate, an idol of forgiveness, who is ever eager to shower His grace on us, but we mortals are incompetent to gather this grace because we are in a form and the Lord is formless and omnipresent. To bridge the gap between the unlimited God and the limited body, the Lord incarnated as a saint. He grants us concessions by Himself adorning a mortal coil. As a saint He slowly removes the intoxication of Maya through His leelas, hence introducing us to the light within.

Saints are the means who carry us to the Lord's abode, the door of liberation; or in other words, they release us from the bodily feel, as they take our bodily self on their own body, hence bathing us in the light of the Lord and filling us with *Aatmic Anand* (joy of the soul). The Saints have actually come to introduce us to our own self. They have appeared to grant us Karmic concessions, by bearing the effects of our misdeeds on their own body and hence enabling a quick progress of the soul to be one with its own base, the Lord Almighty.

Saints play many leelas for our *aatmic* elation, behaving and moving like ordinary mortals. Actually these leelas are divine indications for all of us, which we have to understand and unfurl, as divinity in the form of our soul is always a part of us.

Delusive Maya plays its part here too. When the Lord God dwells in all—an ordinary being as well as a saint—then what is the difference between the two? Simple, we all may look the same outwardly but ordinary beings are the ones who carry a speck of grain (soul) while the Saint carries the entire creation, bound in the mortal coil. Maya easily engulfs a speck but the mortal coil adorned by a saint is unable to conceal the entire creation within itself. We mortals are basically the body, living because of a speck of the Lord, as soul, is within us, while a Saint is the Lord Himself who has bound Himself to a body as an incarnation, wholly and basically for our upliftment.

Outwardly Saints seem just as ordinary beings but they carry the entire creation within. Since the body has its own limitations it is unable to conceal that omnipresent Lord within, so the Godly aspect presents itself over and over again due to the smallness of the body. Saints, while living in a mortal coil and doing bodily deeds are actually granting God's Divine messages, for us to understand and imbibe. God in His own extraordinary ways elates us from the dark night of Maya to the divine sparkling light of the Lord that exists inside us. Only through simple deeds the Saints show us greater, illuminated and divine horizons, filling our lives with a new light.

Saints are the connection that binds the devotee to the Lord. Their one hand is in the Lord's hand and the other is holding the devotee as though one is holding the sky and the other is stationed on the earth, so that the two ends can meet and be one. Saints are the wires that carry the energy from its source to the outlet. The divine flow passes through the wires to reach the button which is still off, that is, the divine light within us. They help this switched off button to be switched on, so that the divine light within us starts glowing and illuminating. This divine light was always inside us, enclosed in the bulb, or in other words the capability to spread light was internally trapped inside this switched off bulb, but because of the effect of Maya this bulb was never switched on, hence causing innumerable hindrances for the flow of divinity to reach us and therefore enabling the bulb to realise the light trapped inside. Sai, our Saint father, incarnated for our sake so that the switched off bulb, full of divine power inside us, could get a direct connection to the source. To establish this fact to the fullest that the Lord is truth and it's by the grace of His representative, that is, a saint, that the divine flow starts flowing in lifeless wires from the source, that is, the Lord to the devotee, to illuminate the bulb that is full of divine light. Sai incarnated to switch on this bulb, us mortals, that was dormant due to the effect of Maya or *agyaanta* (ignorance).

Our Saint father merely removes the veil of Maya, unveiling the divine glory of the Lord and initiating the divinity in our life, to be able to spread from there, so that the divinity within us shines to ultimately merge in the Lord Almighty and we attain *Moksha* (deliverance) or Mukti.

Shri Sai Leela (Shirdi), May–June 2010

3

Immortal Incarnation

Sāīnātha Guru Māze āī, Majalā thāva dyāvā pāyī.
Dattārāja Guru māze āī, Majalā thāva dyāvā pāyī.

We may call you Datta or Sai, but you alone are our *aai* (mother); please give us place in your Lotus feet, as it's only at your Lotus feet that we feel satisfied, as you alone are our Datta, our Sai—our entire self. You alone are our Guru, Lord, friend, mother, father, in fact everything; you alone are the light that guides us on the path of honesty and sincerity. You are that Divine Light that pulls us out from the mire of Maya to ferry us to your Divine light...

In every *Yuga* (age), all the time, we humans are pressed by the horrendous power of Maya that keeps pushing us into darkness, and in this Kalyug the pace of the same is accelerated. It's then that the Lord Himself manifests on this earth as an avtaar for the upliftment of humanity, for our betterment, to establish *Dharma* (religion) and to enhance us on the path of spirituality. He binds Himself to the bondages of a mortal coil, hence ensuring our progress. The horrifying play of Kalyug is scary and it empowers us completely in its digressive pace, turning us mortals towards darkness by dissuading us by the effect of Maya. To save us from this digression, to give us a glimpse of His Divine Knowledge by removing the veil of Maya, the Lord Himself incarnates on this planet earth.

Immortal Incarnation

From Attri Muni's Ashram, from the pious home of Anusuya Maa, the Creator, Preserver and the Destroyer together appeared as Lord Dattatreya for the upliftment of humanity, of mankind—to illuminate us with His Divine light and to make us move on His Divine Path. He adorned that *Akshya avtaar* (immortal incarnation) that will keep appearing over and over again on earth, for human upliftment. Datta Rupa will keep incarnating in a new form for our upliftment—as Shri Akkalkot Maharaj or as Shri Pad Vallabh ji, as Gajanan Maharaj or as 'Sai Baba'...

Avtaars are many but the basis, the basics are the same, their place of incarnation may be different but their work is one—human upliftment. Leelas are varied but the way to execute the leelas is the same and the messages hidden in these leelas are spread in the entire creation, varied and resounding in our lives. The mission of every incarnation, every form is the same, that is, human upliftment—each incarnated form of the Lord created and lived innumerable leelas while in the mortal coil but are ever alive even after shedding off the mortal coil—at some places the Lord's Lotus feet speak and at others the *Samadhi* (tomb) communicates.

The roots of a rose plant may give birth to various branches, but each one will bear nothing but roses. In the same way we may worship Lord Dattatreya or His any other form, the leelas will only blossom the flowers of devotion in the garden of humanity, hence spreading this divine fragrance, full of Devotional love on our path.

Try to gather the ever-alive, omnipresent, Immortal form of the Lord in Datta Sai. Making this mortal coil a means, surrender your entire life at the Lotus feet of Datta Sai who is nothing but Divine Light in our lives—

Aisā yeī Bā. Sāī Digaṁbarā. Akṣyarūpa avatārā

Sarvahi vyāpaka tū. Śrutisārā. Anusayā-'Trikumārā.

Aisā yeī Bā.

Meaning—O Sai Baba, Sai Digambar, we worship and call you, the son of Attri-Ansuya (Datta Swarupa) the one who is immortal, omnipresent, the gist of all the *shrutis*. (Ref.: *Shri Sadguru Sainath Sagunopasna*).

Lord Dattatreya used to adorn mainly white along with yellow and saffron coloured clothes. Baba too used to wear a white *Kafni* (a long robe) or sometimes a green one. In both the incarnations the Lord basically adorned white, the Divine Radiance was covered mostly by white, maybe because white signifies *vairagya* (disinterest for the attractions of this world and the next) and is a symbol of purity. Purity and vairagya are the first steps to move on the path of the Lord. If our mind, our inner self does not adorn vairagya then our desires will keep filling us with their varied colours. They will never let us adorn the embodiment of purity, and we mortals will keep colouring our lives in the colour of this world, hence facing the brunt of Maya. In order to remove our focus from the colourful attractions of Maya and to encourage us to adorn our inner self with the white, pure adornment of vairagya, Lord Dattatreya Himself adorned white. We mortals are ever attracted towards the outward attractions of this world hence the Lord gave us a glimpse of white as His adornment in His incarnated form, that is, outwardly too—by adorning white, the first lesson He taught us was vairagya. He conveyed to one and all that we all have to lead to vairagya, which is our ultimate aim. We have to grow with the Lord's name and in His love, hence losing ourselves completely to His devotion— that is how this intellect, our thinking power, which is fully engulfed by the glitter of Maya, will attain the jewel of *Viveka* (discrimination between the right and the wrong) and this Viveka which is nothing but an offshoot, the fruit of chanting His name will tell us the difference between the right and the wrong, between transient and ever alive. By living each colour of life and by offering all colours at His Lotus feet we will attain vairagya—this pious, white vairagya *swarupa* (form) of the Lord will appeal to our inner self. We mortals, while dwelling in the mortal coil, will be fully drenched in the colour of the Lord.

Four dogs that, are always seen with Lord Dattatreya, signify the four Vedas; we have to move on the path of life by making this knowledge of the four Vedas as the basis of our life, to engrave the path of deliverance for ourselves. We have to accept and follow vairagya, which is an offshoot of Viveka that has trickled down to us due to the continuous chanting of His name, hence adorning a good pious mode of creating good causes in our Karmic cycle. We have to move on the path of the Lord by becoming good human beings, hence embracing deliverance, so that we can move towards the four kinds of Mukti or deliverance and we attain the *punya* (fruit of good deeds) the good fortune of the four places of pilgrimage at the Lord's Lotus feet itself—

Haridwar, Mathura, Kashi, Shirdi mein teerath saare hain

Sai Baba ke charnon mein charoon Dhaam hamare hain.

Meaning—All the pilgrimages, such as Haridwar, Mathura, Kashi are in Shirdi itself as it's the Lotus feet of Sai Baba where we get the good fortune of all the four pilgrimages.

Kamdhenu cow is always with Datta Prabhu. Kamdhenu, that is, the one that grants all our wishes—and that indeed is the true or real form of Lord Dattatreya—the one who grants anything and everything to one and all—from the adornment of vairagya to the knowledge of the Vedas, and takes us to the door of deliverance with the shower of His grace. Baba too is Kamdhenu for His devotees—He who showers all on His devotees, always, , that is, His Divine grace—everything that pushes us towards the unbroken, ever alive truth of life, within the parameters of materialism, showing us the path that originates, shines and moves on from His Lotus Feet.

Lord Dattatreya and Sai Baba used to gather food for their subsistence by asking for alms, for which they always carried a jholi (bag) on their shoulder and a *kamandal* (tin pot) in their hand. They themselves used to collect alms, where apparently we were the givers of alms and the Lord Himself was in the form of a *bhikshuk*, that is, the one who takes; but actually and literally the Lord Himself used to collect our misdeeds, bad thoughts, ulterior motives in His bag and used to partake of these negativities, to liberate us or make us free of the same. Where the Lord Himself is the mendicant, then the one who is apparently giving alms is sure to be liberated, as the Lord Himself is quenching his devotee's misfortunes so that we are purified, without any complexities of Maya, to move on the path of devotion, even after giving the so called alms from our own hands, we actually became 'fortunate beggars'. These fortunate beggars were not only liberated from the clutches of Maya by giving the so called alms to the Lord but Baba also taught a lesson, once again, of vairagya, practically demonstrating that true happiness lies in giving. The alms of our five senses, alms of the complexities created by these senses, alms of desires arising from this mortal coil is what the Lord collects in His jholi and purifies us, to enhance us on the path of vairagya by granting us Viveka. The Lord came as a beggar only for our upliftment, and by asking for alms, He elated us, elevated us to the shores beyond—

Kāśī snāna japa, pratidivaśī. Kolhāpura bhikṣesī

Nirmala nadī Tungā, jala prāśī. Nidrā Māhura deśī.

Aisā yeī Bā.

Meaning—The one who chants the Lord's name ceaselessly after bathing in the pious waters of Kashi, the one who goes to Kohlapur for begging alms, one who partakes the soothing water of the river Tungabhadra, and then rests in the District Mahur, O Lord Sai Digambar please appear to us in such a form. (Ref.: *Shri Sadguru Sainath Sagunopasna*.)

While asking for alms, Lord, you never sit at one place; you always keep wandering solely for the benefit of your devotees. Lord Dattatreya was and is always eager to benefit His devotees after searching them from anywhere in the world. Our Lord God Sai Baba too, was always busy working for His devotees' Welfare, as He still is. Whenever and wherever you call Him with love, or when a devotee is in trouble, He appears without any delay.

Lord Dattatreya used to sit under the *audumber* (a sacred tree) hence it got the prestige of being with Him , that is, it was sanctified because of Him and Lord Sai filled the neem tree with His sweetness for human upliftment, that is, He filled the sweetness of devotional love in the sour taste of our misdeeds. The tree may be of neem or audumbar but the fact remains that pure ambrosia kept and still keeps flowing to us from the same. This shower of amrit tells us and explains to us, over and over again, that if the roots of this tree—life— are fully under the Guru's control and in His safe custody, that life is sure to shower only ambrosia and will over and over again put a stamp to the fact that Datta and Sai are one. Let the roots of your life grow and stay secure in the Guru's Lotus feet, is what these trees teach us, leading us to a state of complete surrender at the Lotus feet of the Lord. Bow your head at the Lotus feet of Lord Dattatreya or roll yourself on the feet of Sai Baba, your life will be filled with unparalleled sweetness. The tree can be any, audumbar or neem—you will bathe in the shower of pure ambrosia from both as a result of the Guru's grace. As a devotee, you will be fully drenched with devotional love, in turn spreading this *amrit* (ambrosia) all around you.

Lord Dattatreya is a unification of Lord Brahma, Vishnu and Mahesh. The message was clear, though we see separately but God Is One. We may perceive Him separately as the creator, the preserver and the destroyer, but actually they are one. This fact is clearly visible in the form of Lord Dattatreya and this unshakable reality fills us with happiness. Baba too used to repeat this reality, over and over again. *Sabka Malik Ek Hai* (God is one) is what He conveyed to one and all. The form of Lord Dattatreya were the basic words of Sai Baba, that is, Sabka Malik Ek Hai. Baba repeatedly said this for our benefit and Lord Dattatreya conveyed the message of one through His Divine form.

It may be Lord Dattatreya or any of His incarnations, their place of spreading Divinity may be separate but the mission is the same—devotees' upliftment; upliftment of Humanity; nurturing devotional love; suppression of ego, I, mine; destruction of duality and a new beginning; a sense of non-duality. Go to Shirdi, surrender all at the Lotus feet of Datta Swarupa, Lord Sai, fill your entire being with the Divine light of Nanda Deep, bathe with Devotional Love in the safe secure home of Lord Datta. The Main Entrance of Shirdi gets us straight to the soothing shade of the Nanda Deep and it's the guiding Divine Light that leads us from here to the Samadhi Mandir of Datta Swarupa—Sai Baba.

Let the Divine grace of Lord Datta Sai beautify our life; let our inner self be decorated by His Love alone. May our vagrant mind rest at His Lotus feet and may we go to Shirdi, over and over again to admire His Divine countenance, adorning Datta Guru in the depths of our heart, hence carrying Him always, forever in the casket of our hearts, so that whenever we look within we find Him smiling from there—Always. May we get a feel of Sai all around us, which is only possible by the constant chanting of His name in a castle that stands on the foundation of love and devotion, entirely and totally as a result of His Divine grace. Our Datta Guru Sai, grants us a feel of this unparalleled truth, so that this peaceful feel flows through us, always in our inner self and it repeatedly feels and exhorts this truth—

> Bhū-khecara vyāpunī avaghe hrtkamalī rāhasī,
> Toci Datta Deva tū Śiradī rāhuni pāvasī.

Meaning—You are omnipresent—present in all beings of this earth and sky. You alone are our Datta Gurudev, whose stay in Shirdi is the ultimate reason of our enhancement. (Ref.: *Shri Sadguru Sainath Sagunopasna*.)

Immortal Incarnation

We may call Him Datta or Sai but it's the Lord alone who will ferry us across the ocean of mundane existence and it's His grace alone that will show us the true path of liberation, and give us a divine glimpse of the Lord Almighty, making us achieve the true mission of our life. So while living in this world, going through the ups and downs of joy and sorrow, by being true to each relationship, O Lord Datta Sai be ever merciful on us, that by your grace our inner self keeps repeating.

> Ruso catura tattvavit vibudha prājña jñānī ruso,
> Rusohī viduṣī striyā kuśala paṇḍitāhī ruso.
> Ruso mahipatī yatī bhajaka tāpasīhī ruso,
> Na Datta Guru Sāī mā, majavarī kadhīhī ruso.

Meaning—Let the clever people, the knower of Vedas and knowledgeable, learned or intelligent turn their face from me (be annoyed with me). Let the knowledgeable or intelligent ladies be annoyed with me. Let the kings, mendicants, devotees or even the ones doing penance be annoyed with me. But O Lord Datta Guru Sai Maa, may you never ever be annoyed with me. (Ref.: *Shri Sadguru Sainath Sagunopasna*.)

May our life progress, grow and bloom on the threshold of the Lord's name by ever chanting His name and may the fragrance of devotion fill the same. The grace of Lord Datta Sai should always be showered on us, hence the garden of our life will bloom with His Divine Radiance and may it be filled with the fragrance of our loving devotion towards Him. So we repeatedly pray and request our Lord Sai—

> Kunācihi ghṛṇā naso na ca spṛhā kaśācī aso,
> Sadaiva hṛdayī vaso, manasi dhyāni Sāī vaso.
> Padī praṇaya vorso, nikhila dṛśya Bābā diso,
> Na Datta Guru Sāī mā, upari yācanelā ruso.

Meaning—I should never develop a feeling of hatred towards anyone; no desires should ever assail or find place in my mind. O Sai only you should stay and fully fill my heart, mind and thoughts. My love in your Lotus feet should keep growing. Wherever I see, O Baba I should see only thou! O Dattaguru My Sai mother, don't ever put down this request of mine. (Ref.: *Shri Sadguru Sainath Sagunopasna*.)

Shri Sai Leela (Shirdi), November–December 2010

4

The 'Lotus Feet' of the Lord

"Shri Guru Charan Saroj Raj Nij Manu Mukur Sudhari"

The dust of the Guru's Lotus feet alone can polish the mirror of our mind. That mirror which is totally covered with the dust of Maya is constantly increasing. We have to remove this filth of Maya from our minds, with the touch of the Lord's Lotus feet. These Lotus feet are a form of Shri, that is, Lakshmi. We have to make this Shri, that is, His Lotus feet, a means to slowly reduce the effect of Maya, hence losing ourselves under the dust of the pious feet of the Lord, for our own purification, hence upliftment. We have to understand this fact that we have to cling to the Lord's Lotus feet as the oars to ferry us across the ocean of mundane existence.

To describe the greatness of the Lotus feet of the Lord is very difficult, but we have to move on the path of life by gathering, achieving and bathing in the divine feel, the joy of purity oozing from His Lotus feet, to finally merge in the same.

The glory of the feet of the Lord, Guru, and elders have been revealing their divinity to us since time immemorial, till date.

To put an end to the bloated ego of Raja Bali, God Himself took the form of Batuk Vaman, measuring the entire creation in merely two steps, finding no more place at all, to put His third step. (Lord in the form of a dwarf had asked Raja Bali to give Him land measuring His three feet, as charity). This is the glory of the Lotus feet of the Lord of the three worlds, that this entire creation was too small to accommodate even the measure of His three feet. Understanding the greatness of His Lotus feet, we have to always keep holding on to the same, so that we are fortunate enough to get the feel of the presence of His Lotus feet everywhere in this Universe. By establishing His Lotus feet in our hearts, we too have to become a part of this entire creation, the way His Lotus feet are. We have to adorn this reality and feel it to the depths of our heart, to the purity of love and to the firmness of surrender at His Lotus feet.

> *"Jya Jya Thikani, Man Jaye Majhe*
> *Tya Tya Thikani Nij, Roopa Tujhe*
> *Mi Thevito Mastak ja Thikani*
> *Te thein tujhe Sadguru paaye Donhi."*

Meaning—Wherever my mind goes,
   Sadguru I should find your
   Form there itself.
   Wherever I bow my head,
   O Sadguru, I should find your Lotus feet there itself, that is, everywhere.

God is omnipresent. He is an integral part of each atom, each incoming and outgoing breath, each relationship in fact. He is an integral part of every animate and inanimate thing. O my dear Sadguru bless me, that in front of whomsoever I bow my head I get the feel of your Lotus feet, the unparalleled joy of the feel of your Lotus feet, which will ferry me to the shores beyond! The presence of your omnipresent Lotus feet should touch my heart in such a way that in every aspect of life, in every joy, every touch, every feel, the purity of the pious Ganges flowing from your feet should always touch me from within and the feel of the softness of these feet should be inherent within me, always. Every second, minute in each relationship, in all beginnings, at all ends, your Lotus feet should be my permanent companion. The satiation of your pure, pious grace should be stationed in my life, flowing ceaselessly.

The magical touch of the Lotus feet of the Lord made Ahilya rise to a living form; she attained the human form from a stone form, that is, she got life though she had become lifeless—a stone. When a lifeless stone can get life by the touch of your Lotus feet imagine if we humans hold onto your feet with a true heart and with full firmness, then we too can surely cross the threshold of life, hence merging into you and achieving Moksha. That is why it is said:

> "*Dhyan mulam Gurura (Guru's) Murti,*
> *Pooja mulam Gurura (Guru's) Padam.*
>
> *Mantra mulam Gurura (Guru's) Vakyam,*
> *Mukti mulam Gurura (Guru's) Kripa.*

Meaning—The basis of our worship are the Guru's feet and by worshipping the same, by always keeping them in our thoughts, and by taking the Guru's order as our mantra, we can attain Salvation, by God's grace.

So to offer worship to Him, God has placed us at His Lotus feet, showing us the upward path of salvation from here itself. The Lord has stationed peace at His feet which is the resting place for all the restlessness of life. To put to rest all vagarance, the Lord has granted us the *tirath* (pure water) of His Lotus feet, hence satiating our inner self so that we can move towards salvation while treading the path of devotion.

When we bow our head at the feet of the Lord, the most essential part of the human body, that is, our head, the controller of all other organs, the station of all positivity and negativity, the controller of our body and mind, bows down at the feet of the Lord, hence getting the divine touch of the Lord's feet. If the head or the controller itself bathes in purity then surely the Ganges flowing from His Lotus feet will wash away all our sins, hence enhancing us towards the true mission of our life which is of self-realisation. This message Baba gave us clearly when Das Guru Maharaj got the joy of bathing in the Prayaga, when the Ganga and Yamuna started flowing from Baba's toes.

In this world we touch the feet of our Gurus and elders as a mark of respect and they place their hand of blessing on our heads. Even in this bodily coil the way of giving respect to our elders is by touching their feet. Probably the Lord wants to convey that if I make you sit on my head the fear of falling down always persists; if you are in my lap then you might develop a sense of ego, as though we are the best, but if we bow at His feet we are free from the fear of falling nor is there any doubt of going off track, as the Lord's Lotus feet are always stationed on the ground, probably to convey to all that the way His feet are getting the touch of dust on the earth, it is an indication for us that one day our mortal coil too will be one with the dust beneath the feet. This mortal coil will one day merge into the soil, the same soil on which we are standing with our head held high; the same head that is growing on the ego of me and mine. Our constant contact with the dust through our feet constantly keeps showing us a mirror of our reality, which is death; it keeps introducing the egoistic human beings, who make big mansions for themselves, that our true identity is this soil, the earth. Whenever we start flying due to our ego we should look at our feet; the touch of dust on our feet will immediately save us from falling due to our false ego and will give us a real glimpse of the true end of this mortal coil—death.

So it's our own feet that give us the first lesson of life, that we are mere dust, this mortal coil of ours. When we touch the feet of our elders and revered people, we learn a lesson of being polite and to give respect to all, while dwelling in this body. Our inner self rises to an outer humble self; a stiff, egoistic exterior further increases the veil of Maya around the true inner self, that is the Lord. Just as smoke always rises upwards, in the same way, we too in our spiritual lives have to start from the feet of the Lord and raise ourselves slowly to greater heights by His grace. We have to shed the dirt, characteristic of Maya from our inner self, with the power of His Lotus feet, filling it with Godly light, to progress and achieve the ultimate destination of spirituality or liberation. The greatness of a Guru's feet is indescribable. Kabir ji has repeatedly sung its praise thus:

"Guru Govind Dou Khade

Kake Lagoon Paanv.

Balihari Guru Aapne

Jin Govind diyo bataye."

Guru and Govind are one. It's the Lord Almighty Himself who manifests as our Guru, makes His devotee grow in His own love to make him reach His true form, by the grace of His Lotus feet. When we bow our head at His Lotus feet it signifies 'complete surrender'. When we offer flowers, it is as though we lay all our joys at His feet, when we wash His feet with the water of tears, in the true sense we are purifying our inner self, hence getting rid of our *paap* (misdeeds). When we offer incense at His Lotus feet it's as though we turn all the fragrance of our life towards Him, by applying *bukka* (black powder), turmeric, *chandan* (sandalwood powder), we pour all the colours of our life at His feet. Then, when we touch His feet with love, we find our life moving towards devotion, liberation; to the omnipresent form of God, by His grace alone. The slave of His feet—Maya—tries to dissuade us over and over again, hence, putting us off-track. All the same, while running in the race of life, which is purely a creation of Maya, we have to keep dedicating all that we do at His Lotus feet. Our surrender should be complete and without any doubt, hence filling our surrender with devotion, love and selfless fullness, completeness, washing the Lord's feet with the water of love flowing from our eyes and taking the dust from His feet as our aim. Only then can we cross the ocean of mundane existence by reducing the effect of Maya, hence understanding the true form of the Lord.

Even while being slaves of Lakshmi (Maya) we fools could not understand that why did the Lord reserve His feet for Lakshmi? When the Lord created this entire creation, Maya immediately enslaved it. But Lakshmi could never separate itself from His Lotus feet. When Maya itself—who befools this entire creation, cannot leave His feet, then why are we not able to understand the true greatness of these Lotus feet. By giving place to Shri or Lakshmi at His Lotus feet, God is telling us that Maya itself and all beings created from this Maya can find the path of their deliverance from these feet alone. When Maya itself does not leave the Lord's feet and stays stuck to His feet, then why is this mortal being not able to understand the same? Maya always gets a high status while being stuck to the Lord always, as it has fixed its permanent place at His Lotus feet. In the same way we humans are born of Maya, from the Lord's feet, are a creation of Maya, and are able to sustain on Maya and ultimately merge into Maya. To achieve the Lord we have to pave our path from His feet, because directly one cannot be made to sit on one's head or get a caress of the arms. To reach to the top, that is, to attain Moksha we have to make Maya a means and without entangling ourselves with it we have to achieve the Lord.

The "Lotus Feet" of the Lord

Maya dwells at the Lord's feet, hence it's His Lotus feet that pave our path of deliverance, as we humans, who are born from this *Shri* (Maya), grow in this Maya, so we have to ultimately find our deliverance through this Shri to reach the Shri Pati, that is, the Lord God.

Just as there is a main gate to enter any place, in the same way to achieve God, the main gate is His Lotus feet. We have to make Maya and its offshoots a means to achieve the Lord without getting entangled in the web of Maya, which is seated at this gate. The only way to reach God is by holding to His feet, where the medium to achieve Him is available that is, Maya in the form of our body. We have to understand and realise the aim of the human body, that is, deliverance; we have to achieve the Lord within. We don't have to spin in a cycle of birth–rebirth by entangling ourselves in the web of Maya. To achieve the same we pray to our mother, father, Guru, friend, brother, beloved God—

"Saainath Guru Maanjhe Aai, Majhla thaav dhyava paai,

Dattraj Guru Maanjhe aai Majhla thaav dhyava paai."

Meaning—O God Sai always grant us place in your Lotus feet so that we can grow in Your grace. By holding onto your feet, we should ultimately merge into you. By achieving the true aim of life we should be able to embrace deliverance.

So be it! Om Sai Ram!

Even today in Baba's home—Shirdi—His *padukas* (Lotus feet) and *satka* (baton) are carried in a palanquin in a procession. This is done to give us this message repeatedly that the Lord's feet alone can ferry us across this world of mundane existence. It's His Lotus feet that get a special place and are adorned in this palanquin of life, hence they are taken in a procession as a reminder to today's human, who is facing the horrendous pace of this Kalyug, that the one who has taken refuge in the Lotus feet of the Lord, imbibed the same inside oneself as one's annihilator, only such a one has hope in life, such a pious soul achieves eternal happiness in life and finally merges in the Lotus feet, after traversing the path of life with happiness and peace.

Baba's satka also is decorated alongside His Lotus feet; they are stationed in the *palki* (palanquin) for our benefit. This is indicative that Baba's baton, the baton that does justice but no one can hear the sound of its justice, yet it never spares anyone who has done misdeeds. This baton is also connected to His Lotus feet. The baton does not forgive anyone who plays havoc with his Karmas. Thus the baton too is at peace at His Lotus feet and finds peace and a place at His Lotus feet alone. It's as though its capacity to punish is put to rest at His Lotus feet. If man wants to be saved from the punishment of his misdeeds or from the slap of misfortune, then there is only one way left for him, that is, to be stuck firmly to the Lord's pious feet, to get relief here and to move on his spiritual journey from here onwards from the Lord's feet.

Even today the worship of His Lotus feet and baton, together, explains to us in clear words that, in the race of your Karmas and in a madness to get Maya, O mortal being, God alone knows how many misdeeds you have gathered; have stabbed your own kith and kin in a greed for Maya. You bow your head at the Lotus feet of the Lord, but only in a desire for Maya, carrying a thirst for the same in your vagrant mind. Why are you unable to see the justice baton of the Lord stationed near His feet? This baton too finds peace or rest at His Lotus feet only. If you keep losing yourself to Maya even after holding onto His Lotus feet, or keep worshipping Maya even after chanting the Lord's name, then soon His baton will give up its peace and speak a language that will shake you up. "You, who are rapt in a blind take-off with Maya, to show you your right place this baton will move rigorously."

The "Lotus Feet" of the Lord

Understand, know and hence hold onto the Lord's feet with full love. Let Maya do its own work; you only bathe in the joy of pure nectar flowing from His Lotus feet.

As this baton does not inflict the souls that are rapt in devotion, or the idols that are ever eager only to get His grace, as this baton cannot pierce the protective covering of His grace saturated with love, give up your mind, thoughts and ego; give up all at His Lotus feet and let us walk on the footsteps paved by His Lotus feet. The path may seem long but the loving, satiating joy flowing from the Ganges of His feet is dear to one and all.

The feet of the Lord are our annihilator that ferry us from the world of mundane existence to reach the door of liberation.

Don't get deluded by Maya that is stuck to His feet; take a lesson from Maya itself and never leave His Lotus feet. Always be aware of His baton that lies dormant at His feet. It, no doubt, lashes at the fools rapt only in Maya. On the other hand it does not touch the ones thirsty for His devotion—the seekers of salvation who have sought refuge at His feet. It actually protects them from Maya, keeping them away from the ones plunged in Maya and when need be, protects the pious souls from the greedy, trackless beings. By making a boat of His Lotus feet, the baton itself acts as an oar to ferry the loving devotees from the ocean of mundane existence.

With the support of His Lotus feet it carries us to the Lord by shedding off Maya, by protecting the devotees who long for the Lord. This fair-to-all baton carries us from the darkness of Maya and stations us in the light of the Narayan. Showing their true place to the souls, their true resting place by carrying them from His feet to His loving lap, granting us fully the feel of His protective feet, it goes back once again to His Lotus feet, to once again elevate and annihilate other souls eager for elation, and to punish the ones who are lost in a web created by Maya, a greed for the same.

The Lord's feet alone are our saviour and His baton stationed on the same is our protector.

To end all evil, to protect goodness and to elevate goodness to its highest threshold.

Shri Sai Leela (Shirdi), July–August, 2009

Magnanimity of God's Name

God's name is our bolster; His name alone is our anchor—the name of our Guru, of God alone ferries us from the Ocean of mundane existence to the shores beyond. God's name acts as the anchor for the boat of life that keeps shaking due to our Karmic ups and downs. His name alone saves us from the storm of Karmas and keeps us secure. It's the chanting of His name alone that can put an end to the horrendous pace of Kalyug. His name alone takes us to the shores beyond. The greatness of His name has been seen and felt, in every Yuga from time immemorial. The Lord has explained the greatness of chanting His name in every incarnation that He took on this earth. It has been said that the Lord's name is greater than God Himself. It's His name that acts as a lighthouse in the vast sea and shows the right direction to our boat of life.

The Lord God has incarnated in every Yuga, in a new form to show the right path to we humans, who are always lost in names and forms. To introduce us to our true aim, each time He took a new form, a new name—Rama, Krishna or Sai. Each name was and is an oar for the boat of life that keeps dwindling on this ocean of life due to the effect of Maya. His name takes this boat to new horizons and new visions.

In *Satyuga* the power of Lord Rama's name created a bridge to cross the ocean. By writing Ram on each stone, the stones lost their weight and started floating on water, indicating that to be able to float on the Ocean of Life, we have to fill *Ram Naam* in this mortal coil that is nothing but a stone, that is, we have to shed the weight of *ahamkaar* (pride) using the power of the Lord's name so that we are without our heavy ego light enough to float and cross this Ocean of mundane existence.

The greatness of Rama Naam is so powerful that even if you chant the opposite *mara mara* that too will ferry you across the Ocean of Mundane existence. If there is full faith in your mind, you are always chanting His name and love is oozing from the depth of your heart for His name, then you can clearly see and feel, the Lord's presence within you, always, on the path of life. His name acts as the guiding light in your dark life, which is filled with Maya, to carry you on the right path. Each drop is important in the creation of the ocean; a nest is made by a collection of innumerable twigs; in the same way the ceaseless chanting of His name reduces the darkness of our life. We tend to shed off the concept of I and mine, that is, the ego and in place of that the light of God's name shines; your true identity that is lying dormant inside you shines, with the polish of the Lord's name.

In *Dwaparyuga*, Lord Krishna once again introduced us to the greatness of the Lord's name by playing the leela of weighing Himself in a balance. God sat on one scale of the balance and the other scale had all the ornaments, gold, silver, etc., that were available in the palace; but alas they were not even able to move the scale that stationed the Lord, then how could they get themselves equated with the Lord? At this juncture Rukmini had all the gold and silver removed and replaced it with a *tulsi* leaf (holy basil leaf) with *Krishna* (the Lord's name) written on it. The weight of the Lord's name was much more than the Lord Himself, hence the scale carrying the Lord started swaying in the air. The weight of the Lord's name is much more than the Lord Himself was proven practically by the Lord for the upliftment of mankind. In each Yuga the Lord has given, us mortals, the support of His form and a name in every incarnation. Because we humans are bound by a name and form, God tied Himself to a name and form in every Yuga for our upliftment, alone. The omnipresent was now identified with a name for the sake of His devotees, for human upliftment. We not only worship His form and keep chanting His name, we also call to Him to guide us and lead us on at every step of life. This is also a means to cleanse our own inner selves so that our misdeeds, polluted thoughts and bad intentions are washed away by the power of His name, hence making place for developing a pious temple within each one of us. The Lord's name is greater than the Lord Himself as the chanting of His name has the power to pull the Lord from the creation to be established as an idol in the temple, inside each one of us, thus granting us unblemished fortune and making us capable of moving towards our true aim—Moksha.

Each Yuga has unfurled the greatness of His name and told us that His name alone is the basis of our life. We chant the Lord's name and are ferried across the borders of the body, but the Lord's name cannot stay there even for a minute where ahamkaar is predominating. That is why it is said in Guru Bani—

Haume Naume Naal Virodh hai,
dohun basen na ik thaain.

Meaning—The Lord's name and pride are poles apart and both cannot be stationed together. Pride cannot find place where the Lord's name is chanted and where pride has its establishment; the Lord's name quietly escapes or leaves from there. If you hold onto His name, shedding off pride, you can easily be ferried across the mundane ocean of life like a light floating stone. Or by giving up worldly glory, Maya, and by holding onto only His name you will find the Lord moving from His firm place for our benefit, for us to be one with Him. God is not moved by gold or silver but the loving touch of His name. The feel of His name makes the Lord move from His place and He becomes so light as though swaying in the air in front of the heavy scales of the *bhakta* (devotee), in front of his devotion, which is based on the Lord's name. The greatness of His name is amazing; the power of His name is above and beyond all kinds of power; it is heavier than the heaviest and lighter than the lightest.

Baba has over and over again emphasised the significance of chanting the Lord's name in this Kalyug. He made many devotees, especially Shama, read many religious texts. He taught us the lesson of repeated 'name chanting' by making many devotees do *parayan* (reading of religious texts in one week). He showed us the path of salvation if we merely keep chanting "Sai Sai" all the time; no *sadhana, mantra or tapa* (penance) are required for the same.

Baba gave His own example, in *Sai Sat Charita* hence introducing us to the infinite greatness of the *Vishnu Sahastra Naam*. Once when Baba was restless, He got relief by merely placing the Vishnu sahastra Naam on his chest. (Chapter 27, *Sai Sat Charita*.)

The Lord's name is so powerful that it illuminates a dark path, makes us laugh, makes us free of all fears, removes the veil of Maya, breaks the weight of ego, and turns us humans inwards towards the Lord or the soul. In this Kalyug where Maya triumphs, darkness of pride fills our life, and it's here that the Lord's name enters our life as a ray of light, conveying a message that we are the lovely children of the Lord and that is why the Lord has introduced us to His name and has given us the grace of His name.

By chanting "Sai Sai" we are actually bowing to the Lord Almighty, then how can the covering of the ego, the darkness of Maya, even stay there for too long? The Lord, before showering His grace on us through His leelas in every incarnation, first introduces us to a form, a name that He has adorned for us, so that we mortals who are solely intoxicated by the intoxication of our own name should hold onto the 'name' of the *anant* (one who has no end) giving place to that powerful name in each incoming and outgoing breath, to repeatedly tell ourselves that our every breath is His slave and that in His absence this body made of five elements becomes lifeless. So if we have to continue breathing, decorating each breath with His name then first we have to let the Divine Light of the Lord be an integral part of our each breath, in each pore of our body, all over, as our living force, all the time; we should be filled with His name, hence enhancing our own selves. Once His name flows in our blood and pleases our mind, then the messages of the Lord hidden in the deeds or in His leelas performed as an incarnation of God, will be understood by us mortals by His grace. We will be able to understand the hidden facts, and station them in the depths of our heart to be liberated, hence realising our own true self.

From today itself we should start decorating our life with the ornament of "Sai Sai" hence filling the light of the Lord inside our dark inner selves. Sai is neither mine nor yours; it's the Lord's grace that has been poured on us to subdue our bloated egos. We should drench ourselves in devotion, with a loving self, and with full faith keep chanting "Sai Sai", because that is what will remain of us, O mortal being— neither the name, nor the weight of ego, nor the web of this world as one day all this falsehood has to end. Ultimately only the Lord's name will remain, the *Omkar*—sound generated from the *Ksheer sagar* (the resting place of the Lord) will become our true identity, that is, the Lord's name resounding in this entire creation. We will not live forever, nor will our name stay forever; the world may stop or come to an end but the Lord's name that has been resonating, is vibrant—will keep vibrating forever and ever.

Shri Sai Leela (Shirdi), March–April, 2009

God — An Experience

God is omnipresent; He is an integral part of every animate and inanimate thing or being, but being in a form ourselves, we mortals, are unable to understand His true nature. We mortals search Him in places of worship, in a hope to meet Him, for the fulfilment of our never-ending desires. At any juncture of life the Lord always gives a glimpse of His Divine self to each being. He shows His unending, divine glimpse amid the bells of a temple or prayers of a mosque. We mortal beings are so overfilled by materialism that we are unable to listen to this silent knock that God gives on the door of spirituality. We only gather materialism even after going on pilgrimages and even after chanting the Lord's name. Hence the Lord too made materialism a means to introduce us to His own true self, that is, spirituality.

Whenever wishes are generated from our heart and the Lord's grace grants us the same in one way or another, we are elated to gather such experiences and term them as the miracles of God. These experiences act as our strength in our difficult times and strengthen our faith at that juncture.

After all what are these experiences? They are a valuable opportunity to seek a glimpse of the Lord, that is, spirituality amid materialism and material things. The Lord's grace falls on all beings equally just as the drops of rain fall on all equally; hence, it is neither big nor small, nor is it more or less but we receive this grace according to the genuineness of our call and the maturity of the situation. Do not waste or let go of these precious experiences that you receive from God. Do not treat them as mere chances or co-incidences, instead gather each experience along with His grace as flowers in the basket of spirituality, so that your life is filled with the fragrance of these precious flowers, and also that gradually with time your life becomes a mere reflection of His grace, hence achieving and merging into the basis of that grace, the Lord Himself—liberation.

Take each experience as a step to get closer to the Lord. The Lord is an individual experience. So the experiences we get on this path of spirituality is the knock at the door of the soul, by the Lord; it is a glimpse of that undivided Lord Himself. Understand, gather, share and fill your life with these experiences in such a way that your life is filled with the Lord's grace; His divine self decorates us to its fullest illumination.

Whenever the Lord incarnates on this earth, His leelas give us some deep divine messages, and are solely for our upliftment. The Lord gives us silent indications and pours unlimited wealth of spirituality and honesty on us. For example, the significance of the place where the Lord lived on this planet earth, what was His attire, what did He eat or drink, what and how did He do His work—all shower that divine light on us. We have to understand, gather and assimilate this light, unveiling the innumerable silent indications of the Lord. We have to make a garland of love and devotion by gathering these small flowers of experiences and hence achieving the divine light through these and finally merging into the same.

The chapters that follow will throw light on these indications of the Lord, the significance of places, events and actions, so that the divine light of the Lord enters our life, a life that is beset with the darkness of Maya, thus, illuminating us and putting an end to the difference between a devotee and the Lord; taking us closer to our true destination, that is, liberation; filling us with the bliss of the Lord's joy and hence decorating us with the ornaments of peace, love and bliss.

Shri Sai Leela (Shirdi), September–October, 2009

The Significance of Guru *Sthaan*

We bow at the feet of our Guru, Sadguru, friend, Lord Sainath, who not only transformed a small village like Shirdi into a pilgrimage but also paved the path of love and devotion for the entire world. Sai Baba is an integral part of each speck in Shirdi. At some places in Shirdi like the Guru *Sthaan* (a place where Baba did penance for 12 years), Dwarkamaayi, Chavadi, Lendi Baag, Khandoba temple, Nanda Deep you can clearly feel His presence to the depths of your heart.

The significance of Guru Sthaan is enhanced on the pious day of Guru Purnima. It is as though on this special Guru Purnima day, the ever-flowing light, the pure nectar becomes even more prominent, pouring its sweetness into our soul, turning us mortals towards liberation, that is, Moksha. Guru Sthaan in Shirdi is the holy place of Baba's Guru, under the sweet shade of the neem tree. Under this neem tree, when the earth was dug up, while Baba was still in a mortal coil, a building in the shape of a cow's mouth was found, where Baba had probably performed penance for a period of 12 years, which was and is still being worshipped as the holy place of Baba's Guru. As per Baba's directions the Guru Sthaan, or His Guru's place, was to be and is still being protected. When this pious place was dug up, the four burning *diyas* (lights) were found here—Dharma, *Artha, Kama and* Moksha—which are ever burning in the form of Dhuni Maai in the Dwarkamaayi even today. The mission or aim of our life is to cross these four phases of life—Dharma, Aartha, Kama and ultimately Moksha. All this is showered on us purely as an outcome of our Guru's grace. We humans can generate and hence gather Dharma, Artha and Kama in the flow of our Karmas or deeds but the last and most important, that is, Moksha, the true aim of our life that is granted only by the Guru's grace. Probably that is why these four diyas were found burning in the base of the Guru Sthaan, indicating that we have to cross these four phases of life with the Guru's grace, gathering the omnipresent form of the Guru and ultimately merge into the same and achieve the aim of human life.

First and foremost the Lotus feet of the Lord were placed with reverence at the Guru Sthaan with Baba's permission. By this Baba gave us an indication that the Lotus feet of the Guru ferry a devotee from the mundane ocean of life. One who takes refuge, in the Guru's feet and the one who surrenders wholly at the Guru's feet, is sure to cross the threshold of the vast ocean of existence. A barren land is transformed into a pious pilgrimage with the touch of the Guru's feet. A devotee who is blessed with the touch, protection, bolster of the Guru's feet is sure to attain deliverance.

Another speciality of the Guru Sthaan is that Baba's own picture is shining bright at His Guru's Sthaan, indicating that Baba Himself is the Guru, Sadguru, the Lord Almighty. He alone is an integral, essential part of each devotee. It is with the sole aim of enhancing the Guru–*Shishya* (devotee) pious relationship that He named this place His own Guru's abode. He also gave another message that the Lord God dwelling inside each one of us, our true inner self, is our real Guru. So know, recognise this inner voice and make it a medium to reach the true form of the soul within, that is, the Supersoul or the Lord. Baba's own picture at Guru Sthaan also indicates that there is no difference whatsoever in a Guru and His devotee, as Baba always used to say. In fact, both are one, only the devotee has forgotten his true identity, due to Maya,

The Significance of Guru Sthaan

and this ignorance is dispelled by the Guru, hence getting us face to face with our own true self, our Guru. Guru and shishya are one and the same, this fact surfaces as a result of His grace.

Another speciality of this Guru Sthaan is that Baba Himself got the *Shiva Linga* installed here, at that time to put a stamp to the faith of His devotee Megha, but actually for the benefit of one and all. Why the Shiva Linga? Maybe because the Shiva Linga denotes our true subtle self. In our human life we have to know, recognise and finally merge into our own true subtle self. The Shiva Linga is like the wick of a burning diya, that is, the living form of the Lord almighty in each one of us which is lost in the mire of deeds and in the mortal coil, a coil which depicts Maya. With the power of devotion, love, surrender we have to engrave and hence achieve this true self within our own selves. We have to slowly shed off the feel of "I am a mere body" to replace it with a feel of *Shivo Ham*—I am the Lord God. This too is accomplished by the grace of the Guru, who pulls us out of the darkness of "I am a body" to the light of, "I am Shiva". So to reach our true selves, the *Shiva Linga Swarupa* can be fully accomplished by the Guru's grace. By getting a Shiva Linga installed at Guru Sthaan probably this was Baba's Divine message to one and all. He was initiating us mortals, to wake, to hold the hand of our Guru, to achieve our true self, that is, Shiva and merge in the *param tattva* (divinity which is the basis of all) with the Guru's grace, hence attaining salvation, to merge, halt and attain peace at the Guru's feet and hence achieve the true mission of life that is Moksha.

Guru Sthaan is under the sweet shade of the neem tree—indeed sweet as the leaves of this neem tree are sweet and not bitter. Is this a miracle? This was a clear message from Baba that we should have firm faith in our Guru. The neem tree signifies, we mortals, who are born on this earth, that is, basically bitter as is the nature of neem. This does not mean that being born on this earth is not sweet or good, but when we are born we are full of the bitterness of our misdeeds. Sweetness of good deeds is concealed due to the bitterness of misdeeds. But if the roots of this tree of life are held firmly by our Guru, such as the neem tree being situated at the Guru Sthaan, then slowly the bitterness of our misdeeds begins to diminish and we become a reflection of our Guru by spreading the sweetness of our good deeds. Basically bitter by nature the neem tree oozes nectar at the Guru Sthaan because its roots are stationed in the secure hands of the Guru. The sweetness flowing from this neem tree is not due to the neem but is totally the effect of the Lord's grace that bitterness has been transformed into sweetness of the nectar of Guru's grace. The Greatness of the Guru Sthaan is not because of the neem tree but the sweetness of the neem tree is because of the Guru, the Guru's love, the Guru's grace.

Even today if you light incense at the Guru Sthaan on Thursday and Friday evenings, it is believed that all your sufferings come to an end as a result of the Guru's grace. Maybe Baba is showering the knowledge that use this mortal coil as incense and offer the same at the Lord's feet, in each stage of life, that too in the presence of your Guru, in front of the Guru Sthaan. Holding the hand of your Guru, in His divine presence fill your life with a feel of being one with the Lord, hence embracing deliverance. Do this on a *Guruvaar* (Thursday), that is, in the presence of your Guru, taking your Guru as your all in all, or on a Friday, a day that signifies your Guru's Guru, that is, the Lord, and attain freedom to merge into His true self. Offer your ego, misdeeds, sorrows, pain in the holy fire, which is the Lord's visible form, and once you have offered your all in oblation then what remains? Nothing! Then how can sorrow or pain torture us? Thus the message is clear—hold the hand of your Guru, after complete surrender to the Lord and be fully free from sorrow or worry. Such a deep message was given by Baba to us, by just lighting incense at the Guru Sthaan; He poured the Ganges of knowledge on us in His silent language.

Baba's own picture and the Shiva Linga at the Guru Sthaan are reflections of the fact that devotee—Guru—God are one, they only seem to be different. Here Sai, the devotee, His Guru, that is Sai Himself and Shiva Linga, God together tell us that the Guru, God and devotee are one—the difference being of the level and in the difference of names and forms. One whose life is filled with all three will ooze nectar as the neem tree does, though basically it is bitter by nature. A devotee who achieves a place under the shade of such a tree is actually enlightened, that is, he has understood the three—Guru, devotee, God— within himself, and has attained the nectar of the Lord's grace, hence achieving the main aim of his life. By adorning the ornaments of faith and patience we attain our true self; we get everything by holding the hand of our Guru, as the Lord's wish. O human, understand that you alone are the devotee, you yourself are your Guru, and God is not different from you. Just shed off Maya and realise this fact, as a devotee; recognise the Guru within you in the form of your soul and in this pious moment of self-realisation, make an attempt to distribute the ambrosia of love flowing from this tree of life, to one and all.

So be it! Om Sai Ram!

Surrender your life fully to your Guru, Sadguru, Lord, Sai and then see how He liberates you from the bitterness of misdeeds by giving you the fruit of your good deeds. He will fill you with His own sweetness so that ultimately there is no individual identity of your own; instead you became a mere reflection of your Guru. You automatically become His reflection, if you are fully drenched in devotion, with complete surrender. See your life as truly achieving its goal, when people stop identifying you as merely a form and instead see you as the one who is fully linked with Sai.

As they take Sai's name, instantaneously the name of His reflection, His devotee emerges. As one thinks of Sai, you too are seen around Him. This is the Guru's greatness; this is His divine task that He removes the identity of a devotee, granting him His own identity, His own true self and grants him the pride of merging into the Lord. He alone carries him from being a devotee to the Guru and ultimately merges him into the Lord within; a feel of *Shivo Ham* is fully showered. The journey of a devotee to the Lord is covered easily with the Guru's grace.

Shri Sai Leela Magazine (Shirdi), July–August, 2007

Three Steps in the Dwarkamaayi and the Samadhi Mandir

Why are there three steps in the Dwarkamaayi? The reply was not clear even after applying one's own thoughts and understanding. Once while reading about Baba's devotee Shyamdas, the fact that Baba used to sing songs, chant the Vedas and abuse while grinding wheat in His hand mill came to light. While reading this fact, the strings within played on their own and the deep significance of the three steps surfaced. When the Lord's or the Guru's grace is showered on us, all knots seem to open, easily and automatically. The fact of the three seemed to dissolve inside, on its own. What Baba got to light, we will try to bring the same into words. I have full faith that His grace alone will unfurl this hidden reality.

Firstly by the process of grinding Baba tried to explain, "I control this entire universe, like I move this hand mill and you all are spinning in this movement. You are moving from one form to another, that is from one life to the other in search of the truth—Me."

Then Baba opened the mystery of three that is an integral part of this universe. While churning wheat in the hand mill, His singing, chanting of Vedas and showering abuses are like the three stages of life that He has bestowed on us. He has divided this creation into three divisions, He has concealed the truth of the entire creation in these three divisions:

(a) First—singing songs signifies normal human life, it signifies the flow of life.

(b) Second—chanting of the Vedas signifies spirituality and purity and that we all have to increase this aspect to make it a means for our own deliverance.

(c) Third—abusing signifies the lower stages of life—it highlights our misdeeds and shortcomings—that we have to shed off, offer them at the Guru's feet after grinding them to nothing.

In a nutshell, Baba has divided this entire creation into three parts—upper, normal and lower which He has brought to light while grinding at the hand mill, "I not only create, but I take care of all the stages of your life, saving you from a lower one and placing you in an upper one."

Baba further unfurled this bag of three through many creations, many stages, many situations; He spoke of the hidden reality of all three in His silent words—

"First of all I divided my own undivided self as Brahma, Vishnu and Mahesha for the creation, sustenance and destruction of this entire creation. I have made this division of three as the basis of all creation. Even though I am indivisible I was seen as three—Brahma, Vishnu, Mahesha, the names I assigned to myself."

The channel of three moved further, by creating three main creations, hence this creation progressed—Demi Gods were the upper link, devils the lower one and we humans were placed in the balanced, middle path. He assigned the work to each soul to move from one strata, as a soul to another but the chance of deliverance was given only to the middle path, to us humans.

Further in the creation of this earth the division of three continued—sky, underground and the earth. The sky was above us, the earth was in the balanced zone and the underground lower part was not visible. Here too, in our

Karmic cycle, three strata came forth. Some flew in the sky while some were embedded underground, but we humans were again put on firm grounds of this earth so that neither could we fly nor were we lost in the dumps but would live in the flow of life to pave the path of deliverance with complete honesty and integrity.

The Lord's creation moved further; now the fact of three started moving with us; on this path of life we as humans could live in three divisions—either we were awake or asleep or else dead. Once again in the sleep stage, since we were unaware of this mortal coil in this stage, our inner self awoke to the deep dreams or peace within; death was an end of this mortal coil; being awake was the balanced stage of life and it surfaced as the basis of all our Karmas. Whatever may be the case, we humans could not shed off any stage; if we came out of one, we automatically entered the other. The reasons to move towards deliverance were embedded in our Karmic cycle, which was stationed in the normal balanced stage or in the middle path.

While moving on the path of Karma, our Karmas were also divided into three gunas—*Sattva*, *Rajas* and *Tamoguna*. The Sattvaguna created causes for our spiritual upliftment while Tamoguna got us down on a regressive path and Rajoguna became a reason to accumulate the action-based Karmas. Humans could constantly perform actions based on all the gunas as it was these gunas that kept a balance in life. We humans kept swinging from one to the other guna; at times we regressed, at times we moved towards deliverance and at other times we kept moving on this middle path, constantly performing our Karmas. We humans kept speaking many languages, of action or dedication, while being immersed in any one of these Karmas.

In the rut of Karmas, surrounded by the gunas, living in three divisions of life and crossing the threshold of this three we reached the door to enter a new life or new form.

After crossing the stages of childhood, youth and old age, we humans, either attained salvation or bathed in the bliss of Heaven or were tormented by the difficulties of hell and hence once again came back to this earth, in a new form, either to dwell on this earth or fly in the sky. Only this stage of life was ongoing, that is, the flow could not be reverted because we could not change the flow of life, such as the flow of a river. We humans could not stop or waver at any stage in life according to our own wish—namely childhood, youth and old age. Life kept moving in one direction till a new life took form, after the halt of death. In the three phases of life, we humans again faced three relationships in life. As a woman we mortals were seen as a daughter, wife or mother and as a man we were either a son, a father or a husband. Many other relationships too came in the flow of life with whom we lived and dwelt upon, yet we kept losing ourselves basically in the three main relationships. We kept moving on his path of life taking these three as the basis of all relations. We were honest to these three junctures but due to the Karmic give and take, we kept laughing or crying and losing ourselves to these relationships.

This was the division from the creation of this earth to the human form. Further the Lord introduced us to this division of three in His incarnated form too. Just as Krishna was associated with many *Gopis*, cowherd friends, queens, yet His relationships with Radha, Meera and Rukmini were above all other relations. Rukmini was His life form as His wife; Meera portrayed devotion who was madly in love with Him; and Radha was His true reflection. The message conveyed here was that we, as humans, get the Lord's company just in our day-to-day life and if we take the Lord as our bolster and walk on the path of life with the Lord as our all in all, in fact everything, then we automatically become the Lord's life partner as the Lord is always with us. Even while being in a mortal coil, while living an ordinary life if we are always with the Lord, we become extraordinary. So it is the Lord with us who elates us from ordinary beings into extraordinary and special spiritual beings. Once we move with Him, firmly holding onto His name we attain the second stage; being Meera we cross the threshold of love and devotion, that is, we are saturated with love and devotion, hence merging in devotional love with the Lord and ultimately finding deliverance in His Lotus feet. When we cross this stage of unending love and devotion it is then that we become a living form, a mere reflection of the Lord—as Radha. Then our identity is linked with the Lord in such a way that we are identified as Radha–Krishna, that is the Lord and His reflection. We are then identified as a mere reflection of the Lord. So first link yourself with your faith chanting the Lord's name to get the pious company of the Lord, to finally become Rukmini. Then merge into the Lord by devotion and love, to become Meera, and finally find the power of devotion, as Radha, saturated with love, name chanting and surrender, as a visible form of the Lord Himself. By highlighting these three forms, the Lord actually unfurled the reality of the universe. As Krishna, He got to light the basis of this three in His own silent words.

When the Lord, once again, wanted to present Himself in a new incarnation for our benefit, in this Kalyug, when He wanted to tie Himself in a cycle of incarnating over and over again on this earth to show us the true path, then, with His own creation, from the house of Anusuya Maa, He once again combined His three forms; He once again linked up Brahma, Vishnu and Mahesha, though actually and always they are one. To give us a feel of oneness even in different forms, He combined visually His three forms as 'Lord Dattatreya' for our upliftment. He came for the upliftment of His devotees. He, Lord Dattatreya, incarnated in many forms in this Kalyug for our upliftment, as a Saint. As Lord Dattatreya, He tried to teach us that in every aspect of life when you experience the division of three, these divisions that you have to experience and undergo are purely the effect of Maya. But these three visible divisions are actually one—inseparable. As you can see me, one in Datta Rupa, similarly you make an attempt to see and experience one in the various divisions of your life as there is actually no difference. Try to connect these three in one thread, as the visible three is only an intoxication posed by Maya, while in reality all is one; and we can be one with the creator, the Lord, if we understand this oneness. We can find deliverance in a state of being one with all, though living with and among many. Our elation lies in being one. Baba too brought this fact to light by repeatedly telling us—*Sab Ka Malik Ek*.

Even today Baba is getting the truth of three to light, for us. In His own temple He is giving us many indications of the division of three and its oneness. His ways to explain the same are varied. He gives us hidden messages in His silent words. Baba adorns the *mukut* (crown) thrice a day in the Samadhi Mandir, even today. He is offered *Naivaidya* (food offering) from three platters of food. Devotees get a glimpse of the Lord in the temple while standing in three rows, right, left and centre. Three *lobaan* (similar to incense) are lighted every morning in the Samadhi Mandir that find place in the Chavadi, Guru Sthaan and Samadhi Mandir. Once again Baba has highlighted the sequence of three—Chavadi, the Lord's abode signifies birth; Guru Sthaan, signifies life, where the Guru's grace is showered; and Samadhi Mandir, signifies deliverance—by merely placing the lobaan in each. Highlighting the oneness of these three is the Datta Murti at Nanda Deep, where diya is lighted, day and night. In Shirdi, even today, mainly three festivals are celebrated—Ram Navmi, the birth of Lord Rama; Guru Purnima, the presence of Guru's grace in this life and Punyatithi, the deliverance of this life in the unborn that is Moksha. All around us this division of three is visible. The deep message of oneness hidden in the division of three, is what the Lord is trying to tell us and reveal to us this fact, over and over again. That is why there are three steps in the Dwarkamaayi and Samadhi

Mandir. There are mainly three divisions between life and deliverance. There are three steps between a devotee and the Lord. All our missions are accomplished in the span of these three steps in the Lord's mansion and they also hold or rather in them are hidden the unveiled realities of this universe.

Let us try and understand the hidden fact in this sequence of three, fill the true form of this three within, by the Lord's grace. Look at the three steps very carefully. Try to understand and unveil the connecting link that is ever eager for our upliftment, accept its divinity, merge into the same and attain the mission of your life.

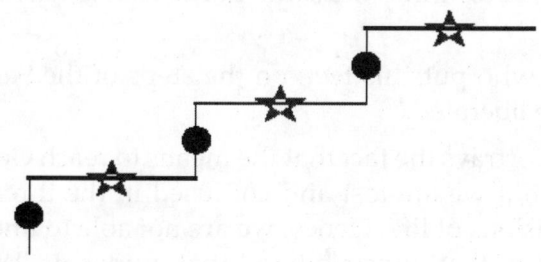

☆ Our Life—three divisions

● The presence of the Lord in these three divisions of life; His unveiled presence

☆ Base—three stages of life

● Support—without which life cannot exist, that is, God.

The three steps signify every stage of life, every truth of life. Crossing these three either we enter the Sanctum Sanctorum in Dwarkamaayi or reach the live form of Lord Sai in the Samadhi Mandir. Yes, after crossing the three stages of life, living in them, accepting and undergoing their plus and minuses, we ultimately achieve the Lord. We are used to stepping on one step after the other but do not look at or understand the link that is connecting, making them stand, giving them their identity that is the joining link. Without this link there will be no steps because their being, their identity is based on these links. We move up and down these steps, and on the bolsters of these links we reach the Lord, the true mission of our life. These bolsters, these vertical connections, these true straight steps signify the Lord; these are the true form of the Lord. These steps give an identity to our being, that is, life and these are the means for the creation of those three steps that lead us to God; that ferry us from the ocean of mundane existence; that get us to the threshold of liberation. They give us a chance to become Radha after crossing the state of Rukmini and Meera. Recognise the channel joining and supporting these three steps, understand its relevance and lose yourself into the same Lord. That is why Baba has said:

"One who puts his feet, on the steps of the Samadhi is sure to be liberated."

This portrays the fact that the means to reach God is God Himself, but we are lost and confused in the three Gunas, three divisions of life. Hence, we are not able to understand and identify that invisible hand that guides us. We do get a feel of the same sometimes but are unable to fully soak its divinity. So live, undergo, understand, recognise all the three divisions of life that are an integral part of life, and try to understand how our life keeps moving from one to the other, at times grows and at other regresses, but we are only able to understand the reality when we understand the *shunya* (nothingness) that is characteristic of the empty space between these three divisions, that is, God—medium or space.

When we move from one strata of the three to the other, we all have to pass through this empty space of shunya but are unable to understand or gather it due to the effect of Maya and hence are unable to stop and merge in this empty space, the Lord. Next time when you step on the steps of the Dwarkamaayi or admire the three steps of the Samadhi Mandir, don't just look at the base but try to know and understand the strength that holds the base. Keep your entire self focused on the same as only this strength, which is the Lord, who will give you Moksha. This is the hidden, divine form of the Lord. This is the true feel of Sai, always near, in and around you. We have to merge into the same and be one with it. This is true devotion, which is not visible; it is concealed but is clearly seen in the steps of the Dwarkamaayi and the Samadhi Mandir. Know, understand, recognise, feel the same, halt here; make this string of three a means and by crossing the same, merge into the hidden nothingness, divinity—God.

Baba has given us many other indications to bring to light the channel of three, messages of Sai in His own silent language—even today three *ladoos* (kind of sweet) are packed in Baba's prasad in Shirdi and the flowers offered to Baba carry three flowers in each bunch. The three is offered to the master of three and it's by His grace that we understand the reality of three, hence merging in the silence—nothingness of the three. We reach the Divine unborn Lord, even while living and crossing the threshold of life.

Thank you Baba that you granted us this hidden reality. Now hold our hand so that we merge into this divinity, shower your grace and give us place in your Lotus feet, so that we merge in the same.

Keep your entire self focused on the Lord. How you step on these steps will be fully taken care of by Him. He will ferry you across, by His grace, hence, merging you in His own self.

Shri Sai Leela (Shirdi), September–October 2008

9

Baba's resting in the Dwarkamaayi and the Chavadi

The journey from Dwarkamaayi to Chavadi signifies the path from the Guru's lap to the Lotus feet of the Lord.

When the Lord incarnates on this earth as a Saint, He guides the disillusioned beings and shows them the path of devotion. The Saints show us the true direction of our life and try to once again connect us to the true mission of our life—Moksha. The land where they incarnate is called their *Karma Bhoomi*. The deeds they perform on this Karma Bhoomi are the leelas, for our benefit—hence introducing us to our true selves. They turn the direction of our life, amid Maya, towards the Lord of Maya—Narayan.

When Baba came to Shirdi, He made a dilapidated mosque His home—the pious home that is called Dwarkamaayi today. Dwarkamaayi—the mother, the aayi, who makes Her children sit in Her lap, hence taking away all their sorrows. The pious mother, by the shower of Her loving grace, gives Her children, us mortal beings, peace, contentment, filled with joy, fearlessness, as we are being tormented by the burning embers of Maya.

While our Saint God Sai lived in Shirdi, He used to rest on alternate nights in the Dwarkamaayi and the Chavadi. Chavadi is that place in a village where people sit together to discuss the problems and find solutions for the same. A place where one gets justice or quarrels are put to rest, is a Chavadi.

When Baba came to the Dwarkamaayi, it was in a dilapidated form, but the place where the Lord Himself resides—words cannot be used to describe the purity of the same.

This can be practically seen in today's Dwarkamaayi, that dilapidated mosque which is decorated today, is beautiful in all respects. By the change in Dwarkamaayi, that is only in its form, as it is the most pious place due to the Lord's grandeur, Baba is giving us an indication that the change, the progress in the form of the Dwarkamaayi, due to His stay, can also be seen in His devotees as a result of chanting His name, meditating on His form and by offering Him loving devotion.

When we go to the Lord's abode we are carrying the weight of our misdeeds, with a desire to get His grace so that our sorrow is transformed into elation—happiness. Firstly, many beings do not get the good fortune of entering the Dwarkamaayi as it is not easy to enter the realms of spirituality. Entering the Dwarkamaayi signifies moving on the path of spirituality, towards God, to get deliverance from our Karmic cycle, as many of us merely keep wandering on the streets, path paved by Maya; we are only lost in materialism; we keep spinning in the cycle of birth–rebirth, that is, 84 lakhs kinds of forms. The fortunate ones who are granted the grace to be on the spiritual path, who get an entry into the Dwarkamaayi, that is, the spiritual path, the ones who get Baba's divine company, love and grace, are sure to get deliverance. It's only the fortunate ones who can watch the show, the ones who have got the ticket for the same.

Baba lived in Dwarkamaayi for 60 years, performed many leelas, paved the path of devotion by His deeds or leelas—at times with love and at other times in a light jovial way, at times He scolded and at times a volley of abuses came to us, for some a simple indication was enough and for some others long stories would suffice. His ways and means were varied, but one truth always surfaced that whatever the path may be for the devotees' upliftment each devotee was secure in the mother's lap in the pious Dwarkamaayi. One either got anger, beating or love from the mother, according to ones deeds, but for sure each one was protected in the mother's lap—the protective covering had been created; our mother's protection had covered us. Now the mother caresses or slaps us under her protective cover, only she knows what is the best for her children; undoubtedly we are all safe and secure in the divine mother's lap in the Dwarkamaayi. We have a sure seat in the car but when will we reach the destination depends on the driver, which is the spiritual car ferried by our Guru, God Sai.

So Dwarkamaayi is a symbol of love of our divine mother—the love can be expressed by a kiss or a gentle slap but we are sure to be drenched in love. You will be given concessions for your sins in the mother's lap—some sins will be quenched by the mother, those that she takes on herself but some will be borne by your mind and body; but these too will become bearable as you will have full faith and the support of your mother's caress, the protection of her lap. So the Saintly form of Lord Sai shone in the Dwarkamaayi. The Saint who doesn't pass or fail you, such as the Lord but grants you the 'grace marks' of His Divine grace. The Saint Guru is actually the link between the devotee and the Lord—His own divine form.

This is the reason that Lord Sai used to work on the hand mill in the Dwarkamaayi. He crushed the sins, misfortunes, bad intentions of His devotees into a powder. Here, in front of the Divine fire, the Dhuni, He showed and will always show us the path that will ferry us from darkness to light. Baba used to offer our *mayavi* self (Maya) as oblation in this pious fire, the Dhuni and then sit in front of our burning mayavi self, misfortunes, misdeeds, sins, the six basic enemies and soak the heat of the same, taking it on His incarnated form.

Sitting in the Dwarkamaayi Baba used to prepare food for His devotees, with His own hands. This task of preparing the food for his devotees was done exclusively by Him; He used to do this with His own Hands—getting the ingredients, pounding, cooking, mixing the food with His bare hand in the cooking pot and then making all, kings and paupers, sit together to be served by Him.

Baba is our mother in the Dwarkamaayi, who not only makes us sit in Her lap but Himself crushes our misfortunes and sins in the hand mill, places our negativities on the fire of spirituality, to be cooked, to remove the ego which is I and mine as steam from this cooking pot. While we are being cooked on the fire of spirituality, He used to give and still provides a protective hand to our true egoless self by putting His bare hand in the *handi* (cooking pot) and hence giving us a feel of His protective, cooling effect, even amid the heat of the fire and then finally used to give us a taste of our true self by serving us the cooked food, that is, introducing us to our true self. Side by side He kept putting the oblations of our polluted self in the Dhuni Maayi and placed the Udi (sacred ash) on our forehead, symbolising the burning of our misdeeds; Maya to ash and the beginning of our spiritual elation, so that we can progress on the path of spirituality with a pure selfless feel.

So our mother was putting an end to our sins, misfortunes, misdeeds, Maya, in the Dwarkamaayi by crushing them in the hand mill, burning them in the Dhuni and then applying this Udi on our forehead or giving us a taste of our true selves, that is through the food cooked by Him. He was putting us on a path of aatmic elation. As a mother He used to, and still does, that is, puts us on the true path, towards the Lord.

Only a mother caresses, kisses, beats and fulfils the needs of her children so that her child is capable enough to walk in step with the world. This is what Baba does in the

Dwarkamaayi. He constantly purifies His devotees, who are full of materialism so that they can move on the path of spirituality.

So be it! Om Sai Ram!

In a nutshell—In the Dwarkamaayi:

1. Baba—Mother (as a Saint).
2. Dwarkamaayi—the protective lap of the mother, His protective caress.
3. Baba's love and anger—at times getting across with love or awakening with a slap, that is, the harsh way. The path adopted by Him was always in tune with our sins and misdeeds.
4. Grinding on the hand mill—end of our misdeeds and misfortunes, ground to a powder.
5. Collect things for cooking—the collection of the ego of all the devotees.
6. Cooking food in the handi—placing our ego on the fire of spirituality.
7. Steam from the handi—the vanishing or steaming away of our ego—I, mine...
8. Putting His hand in the cooking pot—giving us the protection, coolness of His divine touch, to our true selves being cooked on the fire of spirituality.
9. Serving food to all at the same time)—all are equal on the path of spirituality and at times to show us our true face—our divine self.
10. Oblation in the dhuni—reducing our ego, I, misfortunes, sins to ash, that is, Udi.
11. Udi—the remains left after the evil has been burnt down, that is, our true self.
12. *Tilak* is the sacred mark on the forehead of Udi which signifies that after the end of evil, that is, burning down of our negativity we are ready for our spiritual take off; so Udi tilak is a declaration that we are ready to progress on the path of spirituality.

Decorating the Palki

With the grace of our Guru, loving mother, Lord in the form of a Saint, when we are ready to move and progress on the path of spirituality—that all goodness is poured into our lives as the beauty of flowers, fragrance of perfume, with love. In fact we all should do this—as far as possible, we should adorn our life with beauty. This beauty is not of Maya or materialism but of devotion, love, honesty, surrender, faith, dedication which is put together with the thread of good deeds and pious, pure intentions.

When we beautify and decorate Baba's palki in Dwarkamaayi, it actually signifies our life—a life which we have to adorn, decorate with honest deeds, purity of heart, good intentions love and devotion. Once we have adorned this palki or chariot, that is, we are ready and pious, then Baba makes place to sit in the same, along with His baton and the holy padukas (Lotus feet). After being adorned with goodness does the Lord find a place or enters the chariot of our life. The arrival of the Lord is celebrated by bhajans, that is, the chanting of His name, the grandeur of His name and the praise of His grace—*Shri Saai Naam Sukh daai, Saai name ke do akshar mein sab sukh shanti Samaai*, a bhajan sung during the palki procession in the Dwarkamaayi.

The nutshell of all this is that once our sins, sorrows, misfortunes have been crushed in the hand mill or have precipitated as vapour from the cooking pot of Life or have been burnt to ash in the dhuni maai and we have tasted the delight of our own true self, which is the prasad from the cooking pot and we have been given the sacred mark of the Udi that signifies the end of sorrow and victory of good, on our forehead, the Udi tilak and the chariot of our life has been adorned by goodness, honesty, sincerity, good intentions in the form of flowers and perfume. Now when we are pure enough for the spiritual take off, that, inside us in our own inner selves, that is, in the chariot of our life, the

Lord Himself finds a permanent place. He appears, as He is always with us and inside us along with His pious feet and the baton. He is conveying to all His devotees that, "in your path of spiritual enhancement, I am always with you, always in and around you but you have to take special care, be very alert that the negativities inside you, which I have burnt down, should never surface again or find a place in your lives. Make a firm resolve that you will never leave the touch of my Lotus feet, hence the ever-flowing nectar from the same, amid the chanting of my name, singing the glory of my name will keep flowing to you or else my baton is not too far which makes no sound when used" — Baba's baton is silent yet very powerful.

The significance of decorating the palki is that as far as possible we should decorate the chariot of our life with purity, we adorn ourselves with the jewels of firm faith, devotion, love, surrender at His Lotus feet, so that the Lord's divine self illuminates inside us, so that we are fully equipped for the journey that will take us to the Lord's doorstep, to the door of justice, to the door of deliverance — Chavadi.

Wonderful journey of the Chariot from Dwarkamaayi to the Chavadi

Once you have been purified to a large extent and the Lord's Divine light is radiating from within , that is, our Guru Sai has played His magic wand as our saintly mother, so now is the time for the spiritual take off, for which each soul has come to this earth. The divine journey that starts from the mother's lap and finds its deliverance in the God's Lotus feet. This is the reason that the beats of drums and other musical instruments are played with the chariot, the devotees dance, colour fills the air, as today one or many souls are going to move towards the true aim of life — after being purified by the Guru's grace they are moving towards the Lord's abode for deliverance. Yes, this is a very rare treat for the eyes, as a soul, after achieving its true aim of life, that of getting the Guru's grace, is moving for its final deliverance towards the Lord, towards Light. Usually in life, most of the souls, keep burning in the fire of digression as they are fully lost, immersed in Maya. Such souls are unable to shed off Maya even after getting the Lord's Saintly touch, joy from our mother in Dwarkamaayi. They keep yearning only for Maya even after getting a repeated feel of our Guru, His joy. All souls do get a feel of the Guru's Lotus feet but are unable, unequipped to take the path of deliverance that arises only from the Lord's Lotus feet. Even while sitting amid faith they prefer to take the boat which has a hole of disbelief in it, hence they drown.

So whenever you go under the Gurus protective embrace, move towards the Dwarkamaayi, then before climbing the three steps that take you to the Sanctum Sanctorum, try to suppress the blinding effect of Maya and ask only for the Guru's grace from your Guru, shedding off materialism, embrace spirituality, even amid Maya, that is this world, desire only for Mayapati, that is, the Lord and find deliverance at His Lotus feet. Your mother, Sai Maa, is sitting with outstretched arms to embrace you, to lead you to deliverance but make sure that you do not play the trumpet of me or mine even while in the mother's lap, instead try to understand the Guru's grace that has given you the protective embrace of the divine mother. Take this grace of God as your good fortune, hence embrace it with love and reverence, decorate the chariot of your life with His divine grace, move ahead with joy on the spiritual path and merge into your true identity, the Lord.

Om Sai Ram!

Chavadi

Once your Guru has prepared you, purified you for the spiritual take off so that you can start the journey of spiritual enhancement from the Guru's lap, the Lord's Lotus feet, the journey in which your life is decorated with goodness, happiness, joy of reaching the Lord's abode, the Chavadi.

Chavadi is that place in a village where people gather to solve problems—it is considered a house of justice. Baba's Chavadi is no exception—this too is a house of justice—that house of justice where a soul has reached the Lord's abode after being enlightened, purified by the Guru's grace, to get its final and ultimate justice. Here each soul is tested according to its sins, good deeds, devotion, dedication but no concessions are granted here, as those you have already got from the Lord's representative, Guru, Saint Sai, as your loving mother in the Dwarkamaayi.

When a soul, adorned by devotion, love and Guru's grace reaches the Lord's abode, from the Guru's lap, then before the final flight, before the merging of the soul in the supersoul and before the final justice of the soul, the Lord gives one more chance to this soul to ask for forgiveness of its sins from the Lord Himself. This chance is granted to every soul before its deliverance—before it either merges into the Lord's Lotus feet as a result of good deeds, or suffers the silent blow of the baton, when its misdeeds initiated by Maya still predominate. This chance is granted when Lord Sai smokes the *Chillum* (clay pipe) in the Chavadi—just before the arti , that is, the Saint Lord grants this grace to the soul, while smoking the clay pipe, before He assumes His Divine unending form—the Lord.

The true meaning of smoking a Chillum is that the Lord fills His clay pipe, which represents our mortal coil, with the tobacco of our sins, misfortunes and pride, so that He himself can puff them out of our life, to purify us. This is the reason Baba smoked, still puffs the clay pipe in the Chavadi, so that if any trace of Maya still remains in our life even after treading the spiritual path, then that too is puffed out of our life, before the final take off. At this juncture another concession is granted to us, we are given another chance to ask for

Baba's resting in the Dwarkamaayi and the Chavadi

forgiveness and hence merge into our true aim, the Lord. At this particular point, if one still asks and yearns for Maya, once again such a being, deluded by Maya, is put or thrown back into Maya. Such a one does not attain deliverance, instead is again put back into Maya after getting a stroke of Baba's baton. After He has given justice to many souls, who either attain deliverance or are born again, lights are waved that is aarti performed in front of our Saint Guru in His true divine form—arti of the undivided, divine, self-illuminated form—Sai Parmatman. We adorn Him with a mukut, apply the perfume of our purity. It's a human attempt to make the real *Rajadhiraj* (Lord), our Guru, God Sai to actually look as Rajadhiraj with outer adornment. When that individual, divine light illuminates and spreads all over, presenting itself in its true divine form, then in the dark night, mortals bound by sleep, retire to their homes. Abdul too gets a place to rest outside in the Chavadi. Then Baba, our God Lord, bids everyone goodbye, to go home along with Tatya, inviting only him to come and see His well being at night and this divine Godly self prepares to rest, alone.

Once all leave, Baba prepares His own bed, laying 60–65 sheets, one on top of the other, for Him to sleep on. Why does He use so many sheets here while in Dwarkamaayi He used only a sack cloth? In the Dwarkamaayi He incarnated to adorn this life with devotion, for its true fulfilment—one life was used here as a means to get a reward of, God alone knows how many past lives! In the Chavadi this Saintly incarnation of God, Sai, adorned His divine form, and that is why He used to sleep alone in the Chavadi; we believe he slept but actually the Lord never sleeps.

The 60–65 sheets which He used to lay out one on top of the other to rest on, probably signify the 60–65 births, since He has been working on us for our deliverance, have progressed us on the path of devotion and got us to the doorstep of Mukti up to the Chavadi. He used to and still works on innumerable devotees for their spiritual upliftment, analyses the plus and minuses of our 60–65 births and then passes His divine judgement. Outwardly He used to sleep but actually, at night, when we all were sleeping, He used to open our records of many births, to square them up and to grant us our dues, plus or minus. Some used to get the silent blow of His baton, while some got a feel of only Maya at His Lotus feet, a rare devotee, a progressive soul used to get and still gets the path of deliverance, arising from His Lotus feet and an opportunity to merge into the Lord within, to embrace deliverance, that is Moksha.

After putting an end to our sins, ego in the Dwarkamaayi, the Guru's grace makes us decorate our chariot of life and its journey towards the Lord's abode amid goodness, religion, and the Lord's name, on the sound of drums, starting from the Guru's lap, holding the Guru's hand. The pathway to reach the Lord's abode is open for this chariot of life. The forgiveness for our remaining sins can be atoned for from the Lord, while He puffs the Chillum, and ultimately the Lord's justice that He grants us when alone in His abode, the Chavadi, when we mortals are lost in sleep. At that time, that is, at night He decides who will get a stroke of the baton, who will be put back in the horrifying race of Maya and which rare soul, lost in His devotion, holding His Lotus feet, with love and dedication will be granted the good fortune of moving further towards deliverance. This fact is known only by the Lord Almighty and He alone gives justice to one and all at this juncture. For some it's a balance of just one life and for some others 65 lives, depending on our individual progress in the realms of spirituality.

After retiring for one night in the Chavadi, Baba used to return to Dwarkamaayi the next morning only when Tatya requested Him to do so, that is, request Him to once again take the form of our loving mother so that He could prepare more souls to decorate the chariot of their life with love and devotion, in order to reach the Lord's abode.

Chavadi is that pious place where the Lord almighty becomes a judge and makes judgement on the record of our Karmic cycle.

So in a Nutshell:
1. **Dwarkamaayi**—Our Guru's home, the lap of our mother, where our sins, misfortunes are being constantly ground, burnt or lost as steam while cooking.
2. **Journey from Dwarkamaayi to Chavadi**—The journey from the Guru's lap—Dwarkamaayi to the Lord's Lotus feet—Chavadi, once our sins, misfortunes, misdeeds have been put to an end.
3. **Chavadi**—the temple of justice, the Lord's abode where the justice for many births is granted to us by the Lord Himself and that too, alone.

After the justice of the Chavadi some souls have to return back to the Dwarkamaayi, under the protection of the Guru, for further purification; some are granted Moksha, never to return again, and some raw or ignorant ones once again fall into the mire of Maya, into the clutches of the subtle Maya. They are once again put back into this world of names and forms, of materialism. Even after reaching so close to their deliverance, Maya once again befools them and they not only lose the pious self, characteristic to reach Moksha but also lose the lap of the Guru to only wander on the streets, and be deluded by Maya.

Even after reaching the Lord's abode for deliverance they are put back into the world, as Maya very cleverly deludes them. When our head or ego rises, as a result of name, fame, knowledge, or Maya and we mortals, even while sitting in the Lord's abode holding His feet, are only deluded by Maya, then we are beaten by the silent blow of the baton, and to once again spin in the cycle of birth and death, that is, Maya.

Don't let this happen to you and the only way to be saved is to firmly hold onto the Guru's Lotus feet till you are one with your own true identity—the Lord Almighty.

Don't ask God to reward you for the pride of knowledge. Ask only for His grace, while He is smoking the clay pipe, because asking for rights only regresses you but the light of His grace will ferry you across. The power of the Lord's grace has no parallel. With His grace even the dumb can speak, blind can see and even a sinner reaches the door of deliverance to be enhanced, liberated.

Along with Baba's leelas try to understand the silent language of the Lord and imbibe it to the depths of your inner self. Adorn the apparent deeds of the Saint Guru God enacted in the Dwarkamaayi, the palki and the Chavadi; try to understand and unfurl their deeper meanings, hence decorating the chariot of your life with the beauty of this depth and ask for the Lord only, in His abode, so that you are liberated and you merge or become one with the Lord. Try not to get entangled once again in the cycle of birth–rebirth; merge into the Lord in the Chavadi and be liberated. Find your deliverance, undisturbed peace, divine light, the Lord Himself in the grace of the Lord's Love, devotion and justice.

So be it! Om Sai Ram!

10

Why did Baba (or other Saints) Smoke the Chillum

Baba smoking the clay pipe signifies His puffing out Maya from our lives, an attempt to make the inner self of His devotees free of Maya. Maya which has been filled as tobacco in the body, is similar to the clay pipe that is mud-transient.

Baba used to perform all bodily functions typical of a coil and we term them miracles, but actually it used to be a glimpse of the divinity in the mortal coil.

All the bodily, so-called deeds or leelas performed by Saints are messages of the Lord, as Saints are the Lord Himself, incarnated in a form, then how can their smoking the Chillum be an ordinary deed? There is a very deep and divine message hidden in the same, as is characteristic of all the deeds performed by a Saint; that is why all deeds performed by them are not termed Karmas, but leelas.

Let us try to understand this one reality with depth and make an attempt to bring to light the truth hidden in the same. The clay pipe that Baba smoked was made of clay, that is, mud. To make a clay pipe the mud is first bound together with water, then it is given a form to be cooked in the furnace and dried in the sun. When ready, it is filled with a kind of intoxication before it gets the touch and the divine kiss from Lord Sai.

Baba wanted to tell us that like this Chillum, our body too is made of mud, which will merge or be one with the earth at the end of the journey of life. The Lord has created this mortal coil by getting together five components from nature— earth, air, water, sky and fire. He then fills this coil with life by pouring a part of Himself into it, as soul. He gives us an opportunity to be alive after being dried, like mud, to form the body. After many births of being made, baked and dried, do we get a human life, so that we can reach or achieve the Lord and it is with the power of His name only that we can tread the path of deliverance. But this mortal coil generated from Maya is unable to know, recognise or understand the form of the Lord or the soul within, with no hope of being able to reach the same. This is because the effect of Maya is enormous in this mortal coil, and the intoxication of Maya is such that we are unable to get over it.

Our mortal coil is similar to the Chillum that is made out of mud, and our body is filled by the intoxication of Maya similar to the tobacco in the Chillum. The intoxication is such that we cannot get over the addiction, instead we get tuned or used to the same, hence losing many lives to the effect of this intoxication.

Saints remove the effect of this mayavi intoxication in our lives by puffing it out, as they puff into the clay pipe so that the intoxication inside, that is the Maya or fuel, is exhausted and our true self, that is, the Lord's light, illuminates within us.

This mortal coil slowly gets rid of this fuel of Maya as the Lord Himself puffs it out of our life, and the place left empty after the puffing out of Maya is automatically filled with Sai Baba's name. It is a result of His name that the Lord's light illuminates or in other words when the Lord's name or His grace reaches us, it puffs out this fuel, that is, Maya and makes place for the divine self to be firmly embedded, that is, to be understood or felt by us. The Lord's name illuminates within us, for our upliftment, not only to give us His divine

Why did Baba (or other Saints) Smoke the Chillum

feel but for the entire creation around us to get a feel of the flow of divinity that will soon start flowing more obviously through any one of us.

Our body which is the means to attain the Lord is a creation of Maya but all the same this form is a means to remove the fog of me and mine, the desires and selfishness, that is, Maya that has engulfed the soul within. This fog is slowly removed either by chanting the Lord's name or when the Lord Himself puffs into the clay pipe. As our inner self is slowly and steadily cleansed in such a way that the Lord's name, His Divine Light will present itself, illuminating our inner self to be able to move towards Moksha. This is the true worth of this mortal coil—a means, that is a form of Maya itself but acts as the means to remove the Maya within, making us free of Maya and hence pushing us closer to God. For example you may chop off the branches of a tree innumerable times but they will grow again till the root of the tree is dug and thrown out. It looks simple outwardly, but till the root of Maya is not removed, it keeps raising its head over and over again, in one way or another.

So let Sai Baba smoke the clay pipe because our upliftment is hidden in the same. As the Lord keeps taking the intoxication of Maya on Himself, He is liberating us from its clutches and we keep progressing on the clean, clear path of spirituality that is devoid of the intoxication of Maya. When the inner self will get illuminated it will reflect or show on the mortal coil too, that is, outwardly also. After puffing out the effect of Maya internally, the mortal coil which is the outer covering of Maya will also spread the light of the Lord. Though it is a creation of Maya, but this body will also appear Godly; it will be placed at the doorstep of liberation, that is, Moksha. The clay pipe and this mortal coil, both are made of mud; one is filled with tobacco and the other with the intoxication of Maya. By smoking the Chillum, it's as though Baba is telling us, with every puff, "My Dear Human Being; I remove the intoxication of Maya from your mortal coil with every puff of the clay pipe. I take this intoxication on Myself, hence liberating you from the same, and in the process giving you my Divine touch. I have taken the form of a Saint to remove the intoxication of Maya, for your upliftment. I puff out the intoxication of Maya from this mortal coil, made of five elements of nature, filling it with devotion, love, surrender and the joy of my name." It's high time we woke up to this call of the Lord, liberating ourselves from the intoxication of Maya and filling ourselves with devotional love and the Lord's name. We need to give up the unending desire for Maya, recognise and understand the Lord's indications, hence filling our life with His divine touch, loving joy and divine grace.

Shri Sai Leela (Shirdi), May–June 2008

11

True Significance of Butter

Merging of a devotee into the Lord was seen and experienced when Lord Krishna ate or showered *makhan* (butter) on one and all.

In the journey of life, on the path of the Lord, many ripples arise in our mind and many questions hit us over and over again. Replies to some are easily obtained instantaneously, but the replies to some, especially those connected to spirituality, are attained only when the Lord creates innumerable leelas for the upliftment of the mortal being. He grants us a different original feel in His own original, different way, washing the cover of Maya with the pious water of His name and in the process giving replies to innumerable questions arising in our minds and also granting us the capacity to understand His original, divine way of replying.

One such question had been arising in my mind too. Ever since in Baba's Samadhi Mandir I had received the prasad of makhan and *mishri* (sweet meat), which was very dear to Lord Krishna too, a desire to unfurl this hidden reality kept repeating itself inside me. A desire to understand the leela of the Lord, the leela of makhan, from Lord Krishna to the Samadhi Mandir, became intense.

One fine day this deep reality unfurled itself, on its own, once the Lord's grace was showered. It felt as though the Lord of makhan Himself started telling, showing and making me experience this reality of makhan. This feel, this blessing was a pure result of His Divine grace and to share this feel with one and all too is His direction, His order. This feel is a part of His grace alone. His grace is showered on every soul; so to understand, assimilate and experience this reality by each one, varies. Undoubtedly His grace is showered on one and all, but the harvest is according to the quality of the soil.

The Lord gives us many proofs and indications to convey His messages through His Divine leelas. Many times over and over again He repeats—"I am an integral part of this entire creation; I am the Karma; I am the Karta (doer) and I alone am the controller of this entire creation. I enjoy or find joy in detaching myself, that is, the soul from my undivided self that is the Lord; I admire and see myself in innumerable forms, bathing in the play of my own creation, that is, Maya. I have started this cycle of separating myself from my own self and then making myself reach its origin with love and devotion, thus entangling innumerable beings in a cycle of 84 lakh births,that is, forms, dancing to the tune of their own Karmic creations. I give you a glimpse of your own true self, a feel of my divine self, to each being. Some are elated by this touch hence enhancing their search for me. Even while flowing, in a flow of Karmas they bathe me in the divine joy of devotion, love and surrender and through this they do achieve me. Whereas some only identify themselves with this body, burn in the fire of their own ego, hence, spinning from one form to another, from one birth to another in the 84 lakh forms. Even after getting My feel most beings are unable to recognise Me as they are fully entangled in their own selfishness, ego, me and mine, leave alone merging into Me; they are not even able to assimilate Me to the slightest."

To give a feel of His true self, even today the first Naivaidya given to Baba is makhan—the butter here signifies the Lord's form which we get as prasad filled with the sweetness of love—mishri. The Lord is trying to tell us, "Move ahead after accepting makhan, which is my swarupa

True Significance of Butter

and mishri, which is my sweetness of love for you and try to achieve Me, because it is Me hidden or concealed as makhan in the milk of life. My way of introducing you to my true form that is the soul inside you by outwardly giving you a feel of the white soft self that is makhan, is certainly Godly, so that, pleased by this touch, by this feel, you try to search me within you, inside you, hence, making all attempts to reach me and ultimately after churning your entire life you achieve and merge into the makhan that is my true form."

So be it! Om Sai Ram!

The joy of His being, the satiation of His touch, in the form of butter was granted and is still showered on innumerable devotees in Shirdi. How His feel was granted to this mortal being, has been shared as per His orders and permission. How He unfurled the significance of His true self in this wonderful leela is shared here.

After a gap of many years when I went to Shirdi in the year 2000, I was totally rapt with the Divine beauty of Sai Baba in the Samadhi Mandir. I lost myself to this Divinity, that is, seated for one and all. I had never witnessed such a beauty in my life ever, so I was lost in the same, fully flowing in the divinity of His incarnated form. So on this visit He granted the joy of His form, blessed me with the touch of His pious, pure Samadhi. In this trip I was not even introduced to the prasad of makhan. He did not introduce me to His true form but filled me with the joy of His *murat* (incarnated form). During my next trip to Shirdi I was introduced to the fact that we get makhan at Sai Darbar but still did not get a glimpse of the same. My third visit was a step ahead, when I not only got a feel of this butter but the good fortune to eat it also. After this trip someone known or unknown would give me Baba's form, that is, makhan, either in the shade of the Guru Sthaan or in the embrace of the Dwarkamaayi. The last time I got a handful of butter and it was difficult to assimilate all, so I shared the same with one and all, known and unknown and even carried some home to Delhi. God alone knows what He will show me tomorrow but all the same I will accept the same as His order with a happy self. This joy, the feel of our true self, Sai grants to every soul; He gives His Divine glimpse in a different original way to each one. Most of us eat this makhan only as an edible thing, but only His grace unfurls the hidden reality of makhan, that is, the true form of the Lord.

This fact puzzled me too for a very long time, that why did Lord Krishna eat makhan and why do we get the same at Baba's home in Shirdi even today. My mind ran in all directions in search of this fact but ultimately the reality unfurled and the link of makhan from Krishna to Sai was unveiled. This inner feel I am sharing with one and all as Baba's grace and purely as His message. Each one will surely assimilate the same in their own way as the Lord wishes but what He showered on me, I am making an attempt to share the same with you. As per His creation, I am constantly churning the milk of life with Karmas, devotion and surrender at His feet, and in a desire to achieve or attain His white soft, delicious, pure makhan, I am chanting His name.

The Lord's abode is called *Golok* (Lord Krishna's abode) and it's from this Golok that the flow of life originates as milk—the life granted to us by the Lord. The Lord Himself is an integral part of this flow of life as butter, but His true self is hidden as butter in this flow of life that is milk. Butter is an integral and essential part of milk. Butter signifies a part of the Lord that is inside us as the soul which is the basis of the flow of life, yet above, unknown and hidden from the face of life. Milk itself or life is unaware of the hidden reality within it that is the presence of butter or soul. Each one of us has to recognise, know and achieve the basis, the hidden reality concealed in the flow of life as butter and realize that the soul is part of the supersoul. We have to churn the milk of life with our Karma, devotion, love and faith, hence separating it from the milk to attain the makhan for which we have to get God Himself in the flow of life. We have to constantly churn the flow of life with our deeds, love, devotion and faith. By constantly doing Karmas, by holding onto good deeds and shedding off misdeeds, by enjoying or suffering for our actions, by taking all that comes our way as Lord's grace with a smile, so that with the rope of life, with the baton of devotion, with hands full of love and with a feel of complete surrender, the milk of life can be constantly churned and finally one day the hidden reality in this milk, that is, butter, surfaces and God appears in our flow of life. So that the Lord's own self or the soul presents itself to us in this very life and we attain the true mission of our life—the Lord.

On churning the milk, butter appears and floats on milk. Buttermilk or materialism is separated by the churning of the milk of life. The milk of our life is being constantly churned by our deeds, devotion and love with the rope of full faith. Make sure that this churning only produces butter and does not break the rope of our faith. Don't let yourself waver from your true aim (Lord) in achieving the heart of milk, that is, makhan in the form of the Lord.

Lord Krishna loved to eat butter, that is, the basis of life as butter is the true identity of the Lord. The Lord Himself is hidden as the basis of our life, in the flow of our life but has smiled on us as makhan, in the lives of those who are filled with faith, patience, love, devotion and surrender. The Lord shows the path to each soul—how to achieve our true selves and to get a taste of makhan, which is His true identity. Now all depends on our deeds, destiny, devotion, love, surrender and His grace whether we will be able to gather the Lord's glimpse, get the feel of butter, the joy of His divinity. After assimilating the same, are we well equipped to move on the path of devotion, and hence merge into makhan, that is, the Lord; or are we even in this visible form of the Lord only gathering materialism hence spinning in the web of life, life after life?

The Lord also showers His grace, gives a taste of makhan or a glimpse of His divine self, to a devotee according to His devotion, love, efforts and surrender on the path of spirituality.

From some, Lord Krishna takes makhan, that is, accepts a devotee's devotion; He accepts His own self, that is, the soul from His own self, the devotee, in the form of devotion, surrender and faith.

To some He gives makhan, that is, showers His full grace on some devotees.

In another situation He steals butter, that is, the joy of devotion between a devotee and God. But where the milk is burning on the fire of ego, me and mine, the Lord does not look at the butter of such a house. Crossing the borders of love and devotion, filled with the Lord's grace, lost in His divine music, a devotee only searches and aims for butter and moves on the path of life, keeping His aim focused on the butter, that is, the Lord. An example of the Lord showering butter is the Gopis of Gokul; the Gopis who had crossed the threshold of giving makhan, that is, devotion to the Lord. They were totally lost in His love and devotion and in this flow of love and devotion they didn't realise that the milk of life had been churned fully a long time back. They would wander on the streets of Gokul carrying buttermilk, that is, materialism, and butter, that is, the true form of the Lord in the *gaagar* (earthen pot) signifying the mortal coil. Every being is carrying the milk of life in this earthen pot, growing in the flow of this milk, that is, life, entangling oneself in one's own deeds, laughing crying on the path of life and as a result either being elevated to a higher form or falling in the fire of digression. Only some pure, pious, simple, devoted, loving souls, on the platform of firm faith and loving devotion are able to separate the butter from the milk, that is attain God from Maya, by churning the milk or their life constantly with the Lord's name, hence, moving on the path of life to the tune

True Significance of Butter

of devotion just like the Gopis of Gokul. The buttermilk and butter has now been separated and the soul of milk has been attained; but due to the feel of the mortal coil we are unable to shed off the buttermilk, that is, materialism.

Lost in the name of the Lord, carrying the pious self within, that is, the soul, which is part of the Lord, they keep moving on the path of life as they are unaware of the fact that the churning of their loving devotion has granted the Lord's Divine self to them, from the flow of this life. They do not know how to shed off this worldly buttermilk while dwelling in this coil as it is an inevitable part of this mortal coil. They also do not know how should they assimilate the pious, pure form of the Lord. On the loving call of these pious souls, as a result of their devotion and love, to introduce these souls to His true Divine self, the Lord incarnates on this earth. He introduces these dedicated beings, gives them a feel of His true self, sings and dances with them, giving them the pride of His Divine company through His infinite leelas, as the Natkhat Nandlal. But how?

To begin with, the Lord as *Natkhat* (naughty) Nandlal (son of Nand—Krishna) breaks the earthen pots carried by the Gopis on their head, that is, He destroys the bodily self, the ego of His loving devotees. As one gets free of the bodily bondages, the ego is crushed that is the earthen pot is broken and the materialism or the world just flows away as buttermilk. This buttermilk fully drenches us in such a way conveying that this world will just flow or slip away as this buttermilk and we will be unable to gather the same. What is left behind is butter; it does not flow away but gets stuck to us, clinging firmly to us. This conveys that we can never attain this world but the Lord's identity will be our companion always, even after this body is cast off. Then Lord Krishna Himself used to savour this makhan; at times He used to take it with His hands and at other times, He would lick it directly. He wanted to tell His pious beings, the Gopis that the world and worldly life will flow away with the end of this body, but the basis of our life, that is, His own form, will ultimately find refuge in His Divine self.

So be it! Om Sai Ram!

The play of makhan, the Lord's love on the pious souls fully drenched in His love is actually known as the Lord showering makhan or His own self on these beings for their divine upliftment. After bathing in the bliss of love and devotion, some simple, devoted beings merge into the Lord. The flow of milk that came down from Golok as life or representing life has been finally churned by devotion, love and surrender, appearing in its true form—makhan, and, hence, merging into the Lord of Golok. We attain the Lord, with His own hands and as a result of His Divine grace. Then we are able to embrace Moksha, that is, liberation.

Shri Sai Leela (Shirdi), July–August 2009

Shyam Kund, Radha Kund

Whenever there is regression of religion, then evil not only triumphs over good but fully engulfs the very basis of humanity as a result of its horrifying nature that pushes us into the dumps. Words such as goodness, honesty purity are merely left for the books, while these basics are essential for an alive society. When the situation is grave and regressive the Lord incarnates on earth—to quench the pain that goodness is bearing, to end evil by pulling out its roots and to establish Dharma or righteousness.

Lord Vishnu appeared as Kanha, Krishna, Govind of Gokul in the Dwapar Yuga, not only to put to rest Kansa (the evil force) but also all the devils or evil powers of that time. He put an end to evil in the form of Kauravas, hence protecting goodness, that is thePandavas and establishing Dharma for us in the form of the *Sri Bhagvad Gita*. A religion to be understood by one and all, to live according to its discourses and follow it to the fullest—the Bhagvad Gita.

Shyam and Radha Kund came into being while Lord Krishna was putting to rest a devilish power. Both these *kund* (ponds) are almost equidistant between Gokul and Vrindaavan. Gokul unfurled the childhood days of Lord Krishna while Vrindaavan witnessed His Raasleela. We can see these ponds while taking *parikrama* (a full circle) of the Govardhan Parvat (a distance of approximately 21 km), and this is the *parvat* (mountain) that Lord Krishna held upon His little finger to protect Gokul from the torrential rainfall caused by the anger of Indra.

A demon named Arishtasura joined the cowherd of Lord Krishna, disguised as a bull so that He could not be identified. He had come to kill Lord Krishna, on the inspiration and direction of Kansa. Just like other devilish powers he was put to rest by Lord Krishna; he was killed. Now Radha ji told Lord Krishna to atone for His sin as He had killed a bull, an animal belonging to the cow family, actually a demon. Radha ji said that He should ask for forgiveness because the demon killed was disguised as a bull. To atone for the so-called sin, as Lord is above good and evil, Lord Krishna dug a pond with his own flute which is known as Shyam Kund. Then He propitiated all pious waters of this land to fill the kund so that Lord Krishna could bathe in the same and be liberated from the so-called sin. All the pious waters entered this pond, and hence it is considered extremely pure, which made even Lord Krishna free of His so-called sin, which actually was His own leela.

Seeing this Radha ji too wanted to create a kund for herself, which she did with the help of Her friends and they used their bangles to dig the same. Now how to fill the same with water? For this she, along with her *sakhi's* (friends), made a long chain and started filling the water in this pond from Manasi Ganga (5 km away). It was difficult to get water from such a distance, so Lord Krishna suggested Radha ji to fill the same by propitiating all pious waters of this earth to fill the same, but she refused to do so. Then Lord Krishna suggested to the pious waters, which were still present there, to ask Radha ji to give them an opportunity to serve her to fill Her pond with their pious waters. Now Radha ji agreed.

So the two ponds, that is, Shyam and Radha Kund are close to each other and both are filled with the same pious waters. It is believed that both are connected underground, though not visible to us. It is also believed that each kund has around 68 crore small pores and it's through these pores that fresh water continuously keeps filling these kunds. From where does this water come is a mystery.

All leelas performed by Radha–Krishna had a deep meaningful message hidden in the same, a message to be unfurled, understood and imbibed by one and all. Our ability to gather the same is purely dependant on the Lord's grace. Each being is able to understand and imbibe His grace according to one's own individual thinking level. The flowers of His grace that I could gather, I am making an attempt to share the same with one and all.

First, why did Lord Krishna use His flute to create this kund? The flute is very dear to the Lord and as it touches His lips that the 'music' of life flows from the same. This music of life is very dear to Radha ji as she is not separate from the Lord, she is His swarupa. There is one hole in the flute into which the Lord blows—His own self, and a little further down He plays on the five holes with His own hands—a divine tune that is nothing but the music of life. The flute depicts our mortal coil that is filled with life the Lord Himself as it is He alone who puffs life in us in the form of the soul, that is, His own swarupa. Then He plays or creates the unending music of life by using our five senses that are a part of this mortal coil. We mortals totally forget or are unable to recognise the divinity of life, hence, entangling ourselves in the give and take of Karmas and the bondages of the five senses. The Lord plays the Divine music but we only hear the mayavi music generated from our senses. It's only Radha ji, the Lord's alive form or our soul who can enjoy and assimilate the divine music played by the Lord. That is why it is said that you can attain Krishna by repeating Radha's name—*Radhe, Radhe Rato Chale Aayenge Bihari*. We can attain the Lord through His own form inside us, that is, the soul. Once the reality of the soul presents itself to us, we automatically, by His grace reach the Lord, that is, we understand the oneness, the unification of the soul and the supersoul. Here the perishing mortal coil is a mere means for the soul, which is a part of the supersoul, to merge into the Lord Almighty. Lord Krishna loved to play the flute for Radha ji because the divine flow of life puffed in by the Lord was very dear to Radha ji as that flow originated from the Lord's own self, that is, from His lips and the creation of this divine melody really motivated her, filled her with joy. It's the Lord Himself who plays the flute as Lord Krishna; He alone enjoys the melody, as Radha and undoubtedly Radha–Krishna are one, as the Lord and a devotee.

The creation of the Shyam Kunda with the Lord's flute hints towards the fact that we have to use our own mortal coil to dig out the Maya from within, so that enough space is created inside us to be filled by purity and piousness, as the filling of the pond with pious waters; only then can we bathe in the piousness within, to free or liberate ourselves by atoning for our sins. Our life itself creates such situations for us where we have to purify ourselves with our own selves, hence, liberating ourselves of our sins that had originated due to this body.

When Radha ji created the Radha Kund with the help of her friends, she conveyed that the Lord within us works in unison with the innumerable forms of the Lord to create the space inside each one of us, which has to be filled by purity, hence leaving no place for sin.

What do these two ponds denote or signify? They probably signify the Lord's incarnated form—Shyam and His very own reflection—Radha. It is believed that both the ponds are linked to each other underground, telling us that the Lord, the supersoul and His part, the soul are linked to each other in such a way that this fact is neither visible nor understood by anyone. We have been granted this mortal coil so that we understand the reality of the soul and the supersoul and know how they are linked to each other. We must make an attempt to understand this reality to find refuge, solace and deliverance into the basis of our life, the Lord.

The grandeur of the Saints is unparalleled; they are the amazing link who connect a devotee to God. In fact the Lord Himself incarnates on this earth as a Saint, by making His mortal coil a means to guide us, bodily beings, towards the omnipresent, all-pervasive form of the Lord.

Lord incarnates over and over again this earth adorning His *Akshaya Avtaar* ending self). He grants us devotional love enhances us on the path of deliverance, by rning different forms for our benefit alone.

The Lord's Lotus feet are the boat to take us beyond this mundane ocean of life. It's His Lotus feet alone that open the flood gates of divine light for us. It's at His Lotus Feet alone that the flower of human life blossoms.

Under the sweet shade of the neem tree
In the nectar of the Guru's feet
In the satiating feel of *Shivoham* (I am Shiva)
In the Divine presence of the Guru
That we mortals get peace and contentment
To fully and totally merge in the secure embrace of the Guru alone

Three steps represent the three stages of life. We have to cross these to attain the indivisible divine self. To be filled with the divinity of the Lord, we have to ultimately merge into the same, hence embracing deliverance.

Dwarkamaayi is the peace-giving embrace of our mother, where, we children sit, in its protective shade to achieve the true aim of life, to tread the path that leads us to attain the Lord Almighty.

The Lord put His feet here, for the upliftment of humanity. It's here that Sai came with a marriage party and was named Sai Baba. (Khandoba Temple)

If Chawadi is the house of justice, then Dwarkamaayi is the lap of our "mother". From the lap of our mother to the house of justice, it's the Guru alone who initiates us, takes us and ultimately enhances us for our deliverance.

Baba smokes the *chillum* to free us of the intoxication of materialism. He actually paves our path for deliverance with every puff of the chillum.

The Divine light of the Nanda Deep shows us the true path, to guide us and lead us onto the indivisible form of Lord Sai.

By taking alms from our doorstep, Baba actually annihilated us. He used to gather our misdeeds, misfortunes in the begging bowl, hence granting us the true identity of a mendicant.

The satiating feel of being in His loving lap is unparalleled. It grants us the feel of *Adwaitya* (non-duality) very easily.

Samadhi Mandir depicts the Divine presence of the Lord as Lakshmi Narayan.

The joy of the *pothi* is unparalleled. The touch or feel of the Samadhi is a path to deliverance, solution to all our problems concealed in the Udi (*vibhuti*) is clearly visible and this alone ferries us to the horizons, beyond this mundane ocean of life.

The form, the feel, the colour of the Lord is amazingly different, is annihilating and enhances us to the shores of deliverance.

Incarnations come and go but the Lord Always remains...

What do these 68 crore pores in each kund signify? If each kund represents a mortal coil then the 68 crore pores, from where water is oozing out constantly into the kund, convey that our mortal coil too has innumerable pores, much more than 68 crores; every inch of human skin contains 1000 pores; in other words, we have 1,000,000 pores in one square inch of our skin. The Lord is giving us this message that we mortals have to constantly chant the Lord's name with a pure, pious mind while moving on this path laid down by Maya. Yet never waver from the true mission of our life, that is, Moksha, Mukti or liberation. Slowly, with the passage of time and with the constant flow of His name each pore of our body will transmit the Lord's name, till at least from 68 crore pores of our body the Lord's name flows uninterrupted. This situation indicates the fact that we are very close to the true mission of our life—rather the synchronisation of our life with its mission is perfect, that is, towards Moksha, self-realisation or our deliverance. A situation when each pore of our body only transmits the Lord's name, oozes purity like the flow of water from 68 crore pores in the kund, so that we achieve our true self, that is, the soul becomes the picture of the Lord itself. The soul merges into the supersoul and only the sound resounding from the Ksheer Sagar remains—Omkaar Dhwani The Om originating from its source, merges back into its origin, hence, losing its separate identity. All is lost and merged into Om. Makhan Chor (Lord Krishna) played a real game by creating a kund. To highlight the oneness of Radha and Krishna, the creation of both the ponds came into being. Though apparently two, they actually are one; they surfaced for all of us to understand oneness. Shyam Kund is not straight, conveying that it is not easy to attain Lord Krishna, that is, Shyam; Radha Kund is straight and simple, as it is Radha's name that initiates a devotee into the Lord's Kingdom.

It's easy to achieve even the difficult that is the Lord by treading the straight simple path that is Radha—this feel was poured into each one of us by Lord Krishna by creating the two ponds.

The Lord conveyed—move ahead on my path after tapping my form within you as it's the soul that will show you the path and carry you to the Lord's Abode. To fill the inner self with purity, first you have to dig out the mud of materialism.

When all sin is washed away with the Lord's pious name then the Lord's name will automatically flow from within, hence filling you O devotee with the Lord's own divine colour.

Then only Narayan will flow from each pore of this mortal coil, even though bound by the bondages of the coil, O being! You will flow in the joy of the Lord by crossing the threshold of Maya. Filled with the Lord's name you will be ever filled and rapt in the Lord's joy—Divine joy. Getting the true reward of this mortal coil, while dwelling in this body, you will attain the mission of life, when every pore of your body will bathe in the Lord's name.

All bondages will be removed, all desires will be put to rest; all reflections and images will vanish as the true picture itself will surface.

This body, the means, will make the Lord's image, the soul, reach its true home, that is, the Lord Himself. Removing the dust of Maya, your true self will shine. All will be Godly, filled with His Divine love and joy.

Solar Eclipse

When the Moon comes between the Sun and Earth in such a way that the Sun is fully or partially not visible on Earth, it is called Solar Eclipse. It is believed that the sun has been eclipsed. There are many beliefs, schools of thought related to the same—some are based on religion while some others are based on the discovery of science. At times the discovery of science overpowers the religious beliefs, while at other times science seems to waver on the basic ideals, firmness of religion. Whatever the case may be—our thoughts, our beliefs, the proofs of science—all teach something new to each one of us. We bow to all beliefs as there is some reason concealed behind each belief, each thought process. All thought processes, beliefs are based on some basics, on which stands the castle of reasons supporting the beliefs.

For example the Lord has many names; He appears in many forms; and there are innumerable beings who worship and revere these names and forms. The paths are varied but destination is one—the Lord. Each one of us finds peace, contentment and relaxation in our own thoughts and beliefs. For example, we all eat rice but some of us like it in the form of *pulav* (fragrant rice cooked with vegetables) while others relish *khichadi* (gruel made of rice and pulse). Each one is content with one's own tastes and flavours. It has been said over and over again that our *Param Dham* (the Lord's abode) the pathway to Mukti originates from that form of the Lord which pleases our eyes; that name of the Lord which automatically comes to our lips; the house of the Lord that fills us with contentment, which is Shirdi for Sai devotees. Don't ever try to emulate others or listen to what the others are saying, good or bad and without any disrespect towards anyone, but be content. If your inner self is peaceful, full of His name and joy, it is this very place that is your platform of faith. It is the path originating from here that will carry you to the Lord's abode and will grant you deliverance.

In the same way there are many thoughts and beliefs connected to the solar eclipse too, but what is understood by the inner self, as His grace, I make an attempt here to share with one and all. These thoughts are straight and simple arising from my inner self. These are not to prove anyone wrong nor attempt to prove that only this thought process is correct. These are only the inner feelings originating from the Lord within, which please my inner self, giving a sense of satiation. In this horrendous pace of Kalyug where we all are filled with innumerable negative thoughts, arising as an effect of Maya, wrong practices and negativity are tormenting us; positive thoughts act as a balm to one and all, filling our inner self with peace. The arising thought about the solar eclipse is only one such positive attempt. The ultimate aim of each one is—peace, contentment, happiness and ultimately deliverance.

Sun is the source of all energy on Earth, without which life is not possible. So we can identify the Sun as the Lord Himself. The moon shows us the right path in the darkness of the night, making us reach the light, which is the sun. Because the moon picks us from the darkness and places us in the light, it signifies Our Guru. Then comes the earth and we beings, living on this earth who reach the Lord, that is, the sun by holding the hand of the Guru, the moon. That is why it has been said, "Guru and Govind, both are in front of one, but whose feet should I touch first? Undoubtedly the

Guru's, as it's only the Guru's grace that leads us to Govind, the Lord."

Even while being in our mortal coil it is difficult for us to reach the Lord who is omnipresent but we are unable to see Him, due to the veil of Maya. So He incarnates Himself on Earth for our upliftment, for our deliverance, as our Guru. It's He as our Guru who holds our hand and carries us to the Lord making us achieve the unachievable. The Guru makes us reach the indivisible, omnipresent, omnipotent Lord, hence granting us the crown of deliverance, that is, Mukti. Maybe the solar eclipse too is giving us the same message, is telling us that we mortals on Earth, the devotees, are unable to reach the sun, the Lord, as it seems impossible due to its heat and light. But we mortals have been able to reach the moon, our Guru. It's the Guru who will make us reach the Lord, granting us the unattainable. It's the Guru who shows the path to us mortal beings, who are lost in the darkness of Maya, and will help, will make us reach the light, the Lord; and at this juncture in the daylight the Guru disappears or rather merges in His own true divine light, the Lord. This pattern goes on and on, day and night, till the situation of the solar eclipse arises, that is, a situation when the sun is not eclipsed but becomes an opportunity for us to attain the sun. The light of the sun is so divine that we cannot look at it directly for too long, not even for a short time, leave alone reaching or even going close to it. So every night we turn our face away from the sun sleeping in the darkness of Maya till the moon safely carries us once again to the light of the sun bathing us in its light. After many such repeated days and nights a situation arises when the sun, the moon and the Earth are all in a straight line and solar eclipse occurs. It seems as though the moon has fully covered the sun engulfing the earth in darkness, but the actual situation is that the Guru is standing between the Lord and the devotee holding their hands and guiding the devotee to easily see, understand and assimilate the Lord at this juncture, because the Guru has covered the light, the Lord in such a way so as to grant the devotee an opportunity to attain the unattainable. The Divinity of the Lord has melted into the form of the Guru for the shishya to be able to gather, cherish and assimilate his Guru's grace.

That is why the best time to worship the Lord is during an eclipse; even scientists are able to study the sun better during an eclipse. At this moment, this very minute, during this period, the Lord, Guru and devotee are one, without any interruptions, without any bondages.

So actually the solar eclipse is conveying that the Guru is the connection that connects the devotee to the Lord and places both at a common platform from where the devotee can actually run and reach the Lord easily. By proving and understanding the true self of the Lord, he can merge in Him easily. He can adorn His own true self, that is, the Lord easily by the grace of the Guru.

The sun is not eclipsed during a solar eclipse but is a reward that has been granted to the devotee by his Guru where he can assimilate the true form of His own Guru, that is, God. Whenever you witness a solar eclipse, always remember, nothing and no one can even touch the sun; how then can it be eclipsed or shadowed? In fact this moment is that fine opportunity when the sun itself, that is, the Lord Himself is saying—"O Human Being, come and attain me." The Lord is eager to assimilate His own self in the form of His devotee into His own reflection, that is, the moon or our Guru. He is standing with His arms wide open to embrace us, His loved ones. He is unveiling His true self to His own reflection, that is, His devotee through His own attainable form, that is, Guru. So this is the ideal moment to worship the Lord and hence attain the unattainable. The Divine Light of the Lord engulfing the individuality of the Guru is calling you. O mortal being! The sun, the source of all energy, the basis of light, the Lord Almighty has made His unattainable aspect attainable by reducing its heat. He is granting you this golden opportunity to understand, see, assimilate and adorn His true self, making His own visible form a means for the same, that is, in the form of our Guru. Don't be restless, the sun has not disappeared, instead it is fully in the Guru's embrace so that we can easily gather Him, by saving us from the unattainable blinding light and yet attaining the Divine Light, that is, the Lord. A chance for us to be protected in the Lord's protective cover, hence reaching Him, attaining Him.

How can the sun be eclipsed? O mortal being, it is a time for you to gather the Sun, the Lord, attain the Lord with your Guru's grace and merge into the sun by embracing the moon, that is, attaining the Lord by holding onto the Guru's Lotus feet.

Baba's Brick

It has been said that Baba's brick was always with Him as His *sangini* (companion). Baba used to sit in the Dwarkamaayi with His hand on the brick and put it under His head when He used to retire for rest. When the brick accidently broke, Baba said that it had been His partner for life and its breaking into two was not very auspicious. After all why so much significance to a lifeless brick?

Whatever deeds Baba performed, whatever material things He used or whatever words He uttered, all had some deep divine message. Above all this—the brick was really fortunate as even after Baba's Mahasamadhi, this brick rests under His head in His Samadhi.

First of all let us see what is this brick made of? It is usually made up of a mixture of sand and soil, that is, two different commodities are bound together. Sand is never firm and just slips away whereas soil is the basis of this very life as it has been said and understood that we all have been created from earth and one day we will merge into this earth.

The mud or soil in the brick probably signifies our mortal coil which is an offshoot of nature and one day will merge back into nature. On the other hand, sand probably signifies the soul which is very quick and slips away and so it is very difficult to hold it on our palm or gather it in our fist as it just slips away as is characteristic of its nature. Try as hard as possible but we can never gather it to the fullest. The soul which is a part of the supersoul is probably also like sand. Try as hard as we may, we are not able to understand its true form fully, leave alone assimilating it to the fullest.

This mortal coil has been created as a means to understand, know and assimilate the soul, because a body is needed to gather the unseen, the untouched soul. Whenever the soul is bound with the body, inside it, closest to it, only then, with the help of this body, by using it as a means we can understand and gather the true identity of the soul within us. It is very difficult to understand and assimilate the formless. So to be able to know, understand the formless, it is bound to a form, so that by making this mortal coil a means with the weapons of love, devotion, Karma, surrender we can understand, attain and gather the formless too. When the slippery sand is bound with the firmness of mud, then apparently the sand too gets a form, where mud is the base to this form. We can see the mud, but concealed in the mud is the sand too. Now by making this mud a means, we have to gather the grains of sand, we have to assimilate the same so that when mud returns backs to mud then at that juncture the sand does not slip away once again into the mud, that is, does not get a new form instead it merges into its omnipresent, true identity and attains Moksha, that is, its real formless self, merges into the Lord embracing liberation and deliverance just as a river merges into the sea, its resting place.

- Sand + Soil → Brick
            (mud)   (Baba's brick)

- Soul + body → Life
  ↓   ↓
  Aim   Medium
  (Invisible or (Has a form
  concealed)   and an end)

Baba's brick conveyed that as sand and mud are baked together to form a brick, similarly the body and the soul together depict oneness of the soul and the mortal coil that makes it possible for a life to originate, a being is born. Before mud goes back to mud we have to make an earnest attempt to gather the sand within so that it does not slip away once again.

Sand + Soil → Mud brick
(Baba's brick)

Baba's brick was one feet long, nine inches broad and three inches deep. What was Baba conveying to us by these special measures?

Its length, that is, one feet long signifies the creation of a life; one signifying the unification of sand, depicting the soul, and mud, depicting the mortal coil. One feet long depicts one life—a complete life, that is, from birth to death, from creation to destruction or elation. Its breadth—9 inches—signifies *Nav Vidha Bhakti* (9 types of devotion) that each being has to attain or achieve for one's own elation and deliverance; and these nine types of devotion are hidden, concealed and are an integral part of every life. Nine types of devotion is an integral and essential part of every life and it surfaces as and when a life comes into being. The brick is 3 inches deep. The digit 3 is also very significant as it depicts—the three stages of life that each mortal coil has to pass through—childhood, youth and old age; the three Guna's—Rajas, Tamas and Saatwik; the three states of mind—awake, dreaming, sleeping; the three main relationships of a man or a woman—son or daughter, husband or wife and father or mother); the three divisions of Mother Nature—land, water, air. Many aspects of our life are mainly divided into three, may be that is why Baba's brick was 3 inches deep and this is actually the depth of our life, depicting the three divisions or faces of life; those three stages that each being has to pass through in the flow of life, bearing each one and then moving on a life based or laid on

Baba's Brick

the foundation of these three divisions, that is, in the various aspects of life.

Baba kept this brick of life fully under His control, either by keeping it under His hand or by gathering it under His head, else it was placed securely under Baba's almirah in the Dwarkamaayi. This brick signifies our life, the mortal coil made up of mud and sand filled with nine types of devotion, with the three stages of each being's life (detailed account of the magic of 3 has been given in Chapter 8 of this book).

Baba called this brick His life partner and used to sit in the Dwarkamaayi with His hand resting on the same or used to keep it under His head when He slept or retired to rest. Baba only apparently used to sleep at night while the chanting of the Lord's name continued ceaselessly through the mortal coil adorned by the Lord, as a Saint, outwardly. He kept the brick with Him while actually it was our life in His safe hands. He created our life bound in a mortal coil with soul as the life in it, a life that is mainly segregated or divided into 3 divisions and nine types of devotion are also soaked into this life, that is, devotion is inside each one of us but is lying dormant, it is not awakened. It is awakened when the touch of the Lord's grace awakens it. Actually our entire life is safe in the Lord's hand just as Baba used to place His hand on the brick and when we sleep at night, unaware of our own being, our Guru God Sai is always awake and working for our upliftment by keeping us safely under His head in the same way that Baba used the brick as His pillow—tingling or awakening the soul within by making this body a means. This He does by giving us a feel, a touch of His own Divine self.

One brick portrays one life but, Baba's brick portrays all lives, that is, the entire creation, each being in this creation. Each being was and is safe and secure in the embrace of His Guru God. Baba used to and still elevates each soul with His secure touch, His divine joy. He is making the nine types of devotion grow, move and progress in each being and He has been walking, is walking and surely will keep walking alongside each one of us in the three divisions of life. When this brick of life gets the Lord's touch, the joy that flows through it, the Sadguru covers it with His protective cover and grants it a secure place near Himself just as Baba's brick used to be covered with a cloth and placed under the almirah in the Dwarkamaayi.

One day, unfortunately, the brick broke while the Dwarkamaayi was being cleaned and then Baba said, "It is not a very good sign as this brick was my life partner and today it has broken." A few days after this incident Baba took Malasamadhi. It is expounded in the *Sai Sat Charita* that Baba gave an indication of leaving His mortal coil by the breaking of this brick. Baba had adorned the mortal coil for the benefit of His devotees; His leaving the mortal coil is only a leela as He is omnipresent, omnipotent, unending and unborn. The mortal coil was for our enhancement as He is with us even today after leaving the mortal coil. He is with us each moment, each second, and we can get His feel in the blowing wind, in happiness and sorrow, in elation and digression, in fact in everything and anything.

Breaking of the brick and Baba's leaving the mortal coil was an indication to us that our life will come to an end when the two basics of our life will separate from one another — soul and the body (sand + mud). Body is mud and so will merge into the same; the soul will either get a new form with another part of the earth or will attain its true identity to embrace liberation and Lord's grace in this life itself. With the combination of sand and mud, with the coming together of the body and the soul, some beings will make this body a medium and come what may, will not let the sand slip away; and before the body is lost in mud, will understand, assimilate and gather the minute soul and will merge into the true form of the Lord, that is, will attain the Lord before leaving the mortal coil, will embrace aatmic deliverance, will merge in peace, away from the cycle of birth–rebirth.

Om Sai Ram!

Baba's Brick

Baba's hand on the brick grants us His divine touch, turning our lives towards the Lord, purely as a result of His grace. When He used to place the brick under His head, at that time He was actually internally enhancing each one of us by dreams and visions. He used to shower His grace, hence enhancing each one of us. Maybe that is why His brick got a place along with His Chillum and baton in His Samadhi. Even today Baba is puffing out the intoxication of Maya and filling our inner self with the sweetness of spirituality from His Samadhi, but wherever need be He uses His baton too, to put a devotee on the right path of love and devotion. Even today the brick of life is placed under His head hence elating and enhancing each one of us. He is making our mortal coil a means, a medium to make us move towards spirituality. He is constantly making us move towards His true self, the Lord Almighty, by giving us the true knowledge of the soul. That is why Baba has said, "My Samadhi will not only speak to my devotees but will also be active for their benefit as I am 'ever alive' for My devotees from my tomb." May be that is why, on the inspiration and as per His orders His life partner, the brick got place in His Samadhi and through this brick many souls such as our lives attained their spiritual aim, that is, peace, rest and contentment.

Even Lord Vitthal is standing on a brick waiting for His devotee *Pundalik*, that is, He has kept the entire life, that is, the entire creation safely under His Lotus feet. To enhance or portray the selfless devotion, full of love of His devotees, He portrays that even today He is waiting for His true devotee, standing on a brick, in fact on His devotee's life itself, whereas actually He is enhancing and elating us by keeping us under the protective shade of His Lotus feet. He is granting the divine light of His spiritual joy to each brick by His grace by making this mortal coil a means for the same.

O devotees! O countless Pundaliks of this creation! Awake and realise that the Lord standing on a brick, apparently waiting for you, is actually enhancing and elating you. By standing on the brick or resting His hand on the same or by keeping it under His head, He is actually building the protective layer of His grace around you. Through this brick or body He is making you reach the sand or the soul that is concealed in your life itself, hence, progressing you towards Moksha, Mukti and deliverance.

So be it! Om Sai Ram!

The mixing of mud and sand together is like the presence of the soul in the body, existing together and, hence, the creation of a life as a brick. Its true identity lies in the embrace of the Lord. We have to make the mud a means to make the silt or sand reach and merge into the sea; we have to shed the mortal coil at the end of this life, but before that we have to ferry this sand to its true destination, lest it again mingle with the mud of maya. This can be achieved by the power of the Lord's name and His grace. Though it is not stable, yet it, that is, the soul has to firmly embrace the Lord to attain the Light of deliverance. Before the brick breaks, mud mingles with mud, with the weapons of the Lord's name and the Lord's devotion and surrender at His Lotus feet. We have to give firmness to this sand with good conduct or deeds totally based on the Lord's name so that the sand does not require mud once again to become firm.

We have to merge into the Lord's peaceful, ever alive, unending, firm, identity, the sea that merges all rivers into it.

We have to attain our true identity, that is, Moksha, Mukti or self-realisation. We have to be fully 'Sai', that is, attain our true identity, the Lord.

(The description of the brick is an inner message from the Lord and in no way is it trying to say that the soul and body are what constitute a brick).

Shri Sai Leela Magazine (Shirdi), September–October, 2010

Sai Maa in Dwarkamaayi

A Mother is God's representative on earth. The Lord is omnipresent, a part of each speck of this creation; but we mortal beings are unable to understand His invisible presence as we all are bound by the bondages of this body. Even to see our own reflection we need a mirror; therefore, it is not easy for us to understand and assimilate the formless presence of God or His true self present inside each one of us. When the Lord Himself cannot be present bodily at all places, though God is omnipresent, that is why He has sent His representative on earth as our *janani, Aai*—our mother. Only a mother loves her children selflessly with a very pure self, not like the other relations that are based on selfishness—give or take in an obvious or concealed way. Only a mother is always worried for her children. Ever since the child is born and till the mother lives, she always prays and desires for her children's benefit, upliftment and progress and is ever eager to do anything for them. A child may remember or forget his or her mother with the flow of time, but a mother never forsakes her children. She is always ever active and eager for his or her upliftment. She is not at peace till she hears about her children's well being and security with her own ears and from their own mouth. She is elated on hearing the voice of her children. If her children are far from her, she yearns for them, and her joy is boundless on hearing from them.

When our mother, who has brought us into this world, in this life only, is ready to shower her all on us then what to say of Sai Maa, our Lord Almighty, who incarnates on this earth, over and over again, in a new form for our elation enhancement. Our Sai Maa incarnated in this kalyug for our benefit and His house is called Dwarkamaayi—a mother that soaks all the difficulties of Her devotees, burns our sins and blows away our ego, to purify us, to be able to tread the path of spirituality and move ahead to attain Moksha.

Our Sai Maa is like our mother who has given birth to us; one gets us into this material world and teaches us to pave our way, and the other puts us on the path of deliverance, takes us to show what lies beyond this life even while doing our everyday deeds. She takes us in Her comforting, loving embrace, hence granting us peace and contentment.

First a mother carries her child in her womb for nine months before bringing him or her into this world whereas, on the other hand, Guru Maa grants her children nine types of devotion, hence enabling and guiding us to enter the unique comforting world of spirituality.

Second, a mother feeds her child, who is helpless and totally dependent on her; and Sai maa on the other hand grants maakhan from the pure flow of milk flowing from the Golok to Her child, who has just entered the realms of spirituality; that is, a worldly mother gives milk to her child who is totally dependent on her and Sai Maa grants Her first touch, Her true feel, that is, makhan, from the flow of life to a neonatal and sets them on the path of spirituality, one who is fully filled with complete surrender at the Lord's feet. This complete dependence or surrender of the child to his mother, Sai Maa alone ferries him across the ocean of mundane existence. In the absence of surrender, even the mother might not always be focused on her child; in other words would not give him full attention always.

Third a mother sticks her child to her bosom giving him a dry place to sleep while she herself sleeps on the wet area soiled by the child. Similary our Guru Maa atones for our sins, takes them on Herself granting us goodness, honesty, peace, happiness, keeping us very close to Herself, hence making us fearless. She does not let us cry due to our sorrows, that is, Sai Maa overlooks the wetness of our misdeeds and sorrows, and instead showers the shade of Her grace making us free of our sorrow and forever keeping us happy and prosperous by taking all our sorrows on Herself, Our Sai Maa.

As we move ahead, it's our mother alone who adorns her child and feels elated on seeing the well-adorned child, cherishing the joy flowing in her contented mind on seeing her adorned child. Sai maa too adorns us with Her grace, love and devotion, and feels elated, happy and contented on seeing our progress towards Her, that is, towards our true mission of life. It's the adornment of a child, with the loving and caring hands of a mother that beautifies us divinely, hence pushing us towards our true mission—bodily to become a good human being and spiritually to attain salvation.

Every mother wants her children to be well educated, so she teaches her children the basic values of life, gives them all the knowledge to sustain themselves on the path of life and to make them good human beings. She tries to instil moral values so that her child is always ahead and comes first. In the same way our Sai Maa also grants us knowledge, so that the layer of ignorance engulfing us is slowly shed off and Her devotee moves on the path of spirituality, the path that leads to God, our Guru. Our Sai Maa makes sure that we are not left behind in any way. Ignorance is shed off and knowledge shines; we mortals who are lost in the darkness, slowly shed off the dust of ignorance with the grace of the knowledge and love attained as a result of His Divine grace alone. Subsequently the light of knowledge illuminates to the fullest—the light that has always been inside us, to an extent that the Divine light not only illuminates us but radiates all around us.

The child may be close to or far away from the mother, but the mother is always eager for the child's welfare; the child may be good or bad, but a mother's heart always showers blessings on her children. Similarly we may be in Shirdi or miles away, Baba is always eager for our welfare, one may be a devotee or an atheist but the Lord always wants the upliftment of one and all. The Lord surely shows each one the path leading to the true missions of our life, that is, Moksha, Mukti or deliverance.

After such arduous efforts, hard penance and the unaccountable sacrifices of a mother to pour all goodness in and for her children, if the child does not move in the direction desired and dreamt by his mother, then it hurts the mother. At this juncture a mother even hits her child to put him back on the right path, because she is immensely pained when she sees her child moving on the wrong path. Sai Maa too showers us with His anger, abuses or even spanks us with His baton when we deter from the right path and start moving towards darkness and regression due to the horrendous effect of Maya and the subtle ego. While moving on the path of spirituality we start falling in the dark pit of Maya instead of treading the path towards deliverance as we are affected in a negative way by Maya and the me and mine, that is, our ego. So while moving on your Karmic path, don't ever forget the teachings and values given to you by your parents. The flow of time, the thread of your deeds may carry you to unknown, new lands but come what may never waver from your base, that is, the teachings of your parents, the values, the name of the Lord—never ever forget these. Surely then, as time passes, in an obvious or revealed way, you will keep progressing towards your true aim of life. Even in the midst of worldly deeds you will spread the name and values instilled in you and make your parents, Guru and God proud, by your deeds and actions, hence moving towards the true aim of your life, to attain the same, that is, deliverance or merge into the Lotus feet of the Lord.

In the horrendous pace of life, if the child goes away from his parents to earn his bread and butter, enters his work place, his Karma bhoomi, to move in pace with this materialistic world, he goes away from the mother's protective embrace. Though the child is miles away, a mother is always thinking of him, worried for his welfare, and always prays for his happiness and his progress. In the same way Sai Maa too is always eager and worried, that come what may Her children must come to Her, specially, those children who are far from Her or far from spirituality and lost in Maya for the progression of life. The child or devotee may be far or near, but the love of our Sai Maa, the shower of Her grace is bestowed on each one and one is filled with this Divine grace. The child can move towards his true aim, that is, deliverance, though bodily he or she may be miles away. Constant thought of the Lotus feet of Sai Maa, one day leads us to and merges us in these pious pure Lotus feet.

When a child goes on a tour, the mother is not at peace till her child reaches the desired destination. In the same way our Sai Maa is never sitting at one place, leave alone sleeping, till Her child reaches his or her true destination, that is, embraces Moksha or Mukti. Sleeping for Baba was just a seemingly performed act as He is 'ever awake' for the welfare of His devotees and He is earnestly working for the same.

A mother carries a child in her womb for 9 months and is always worried for her child's welfare, his requirements and in showing him the right path, till her last breath. Our Sai Maa holds the hand of each child not only till the last breath taken by Her child but even after the end of this mortal coil. The Lord never forsakes a soul that is immersed fully in His Love and devotion, hence leading such a one to the door of deliverance and merging him or her in His true divine self.

So be it! Om Sai Ram!

Our mother in this life, is that means, the path, that gives form, that is, this body for the soul to enter the realms of this life, whereas the Guru Maa always enhances Her child towards the true mission of life, that of spiritually. She Herself bears the tormenting heat, grants Her *atma gyana* (true knowledge) to its own part bound in the body, that is, the soul, finally merging it in the *parmatman* (the Lord of the soul). She merges this thirsty river, that is, the soul, into the sea, that is, the Lord giving it its own identity, the greatest honour. Before merging into the sea, the river loses its true identity, by the grace of the Lord; the restlessness of the river is put to rest in the roar of the sea. A river divides into many tributaries before entering the sea, that is, it gains its true identity; only after losing its own identity the river becomes the sea itself.

To lose one's self is to attain God. Placing our head in the lap of our Maai—Dwarkamaayi we have to fill ourselves with the love flowing from our mother, bathing in Her grace and hence attaining happiness, contentment, peace and joy. Losing ourselves into the identity of our mother, we have to merge in Her with a sense of complete surrender; we have to attain deliverance by crossing the mire of Maya, putting an end to the cycle of birth–rebirth by the power of His Divine touch. Bathing in the joy of His grace, we have to merge in the Divine embrace of our Guru Maa, hence becoming Maa, the Divine light, ourselves and then merging into peace forever and ever. We have to make this mortal coil, created by Sai Maa, a means to lead the soul to its true destination—to merge into the Lord. We have to attain the true aim of our life—to become the *tattva* or the Lord. Make this mortal coil a medium to give up the sense of I concealed as Maya in the same, so that the outward bodily self too radiates a reflection of Sai, as though we mortals attain salvation even while being bound in this mortal coil. Dwarkamaayi is our true mother, the Divine mother who always showers love on us, and undoubtedly the Lord and Saints are nothing but Love. So it's Dwarkamaai alone that is our Divine mother that showers unending love on Her children and the Divine passion from Her takes us beyond perceptible thresholds of this body to the unknown, undiscovered, unimagined realms of spirituality.

Khandoba Temple

(Baba first arrived in Shirdi with a marriage party in this temple)

We all are familiar with the significance of the Guru Sthaan; the greatness of this pious place is known to all, as Baba said this is His Guru's place hence telling one and all to respect, revere and protect the same. As mentioned in Chapter 7, Baba did penance at this very place for 12 years (as written in *Sai Sat Charita*). Baba's own picture is placed at His Guru's place and He got the Shivlinga placed with due rites at this very pious place, probably to tell and explain to us that we ourselves are our own Guru as the Lord God resides inside us, but before knowing and recognising this Guru within we have to increase our love, chanting, surrender, devotion in the incarnated form of our Guru to be finally awarded the Gurus grace; we have to ignite the sense, the feel of Shivo Ham to finally be one with the Lord, that is, become Lord Himself. We have to move and tread the path of devotional love by sweetening this bitter neem, that is, life.

If the roots of this bitter yet advantageous neem of life are dedicated or bound to the Guru's Lotus feet then even amid the dissuading Maya, the sweetness of the Lord's name fills our life—the shower of Guru's Nectar makes our entire life happy, peaceful and progressive. To awaken the Lord within, to highlight and play on the strings of Shivo Ham, probably

Baba got Shivalinga placed with respect at the Guru Sthaan and to awaken the Shiva in each one of us. He stepped in the Khandoba temple and in front of this Shiva, the subtle true self inside us, Lord Shiva Himself got a new name in the coil of a saint; the incarnated Lord Himself got a name—Sai. The Lord Himself, in the form of Shiva, appeared for our own benefit as Sai and began the journey of His incarnation from the Khandoba temple up to the neem tree, to Dwarkamaayi, to Chavadi, to Lendi Bagh and to Nandadeep to be firmly established in each devotees heart. He became a part and parcel of each speck of Shirdi. He granted us piousness by spreading His divine perfume all over. He gave us the joy of His being with us, He gave us a touch of purity hence showing us the path of spirituality, deliverance or Moksha.

The Lord Himself granted us His Divinity of being with us as a saint, bound to a mortal coil; He Himself gave us the feel of Shivo Ham.

On the occasion of a wedding all the people sing and dance in the *baraat* (marriage procession). Baba's arrival at the Khandoba temple was also with a baraat but this was not an ordinary wedding procession because this pious procession took Lord Sai to His place of deeds, to His Karma Bhoomi, as an incarnation of God. The people in this procession were probably those fortunate souls who were granted the fruit of penance of many births—the rare opportunity to accompany the incarnated form of the Lord to His place of work. These fortunate souls were accompanied by many Gods, Demi Gods as this was a moment to rejoice, a time for celebration as the true groom of this procession was rare and wonderful, that is, the Lord God Himself. This rare groom was actually a part of the people accompanying the wedding procession—to show the true path of surrender, love and devotion to us mortals who have lost our way in the mire of Maya. He came to hold the hand of His children or devotees and put them on the path leading onto Him, to wed each soul to Himself, the supersoul, that is, to grant us mortals deliverance.

This wedding procession was unique as the divine groom Himself was a part of the people in the procession, as He had come to colour each soul in His divine colour. He had come to enhance us in the soothing shade of devotion, love, surrender and to wed each soul to the supersoul under His Divine protection. To show us the path of deliverance by granting us self-realisation.

As we start all our deeds with the pious name of the Lord that is why Baba first appeared at Khandoba temple (the temple of the Lord) and in front of His own Godly self (Lord Shiva) gave recognition to His incarnated form as Sai, that is, Lord God Himself. For the upliftment of us foolish mortals, He bound Himself not only to a form but to a name too. The leelas of this incarnation started from here itself, which shone not only under the neem tree but spread to entire Shirdi; in fact everywhere. Within no lime these leelas played on the inner strings of each being, hence adorning one and all with love and devotion, and enhancing all on the path of spiritual deliverance.

Each atom, each speck of Shirdi is pure and pious; each stone, every grain of mud has the feel, the touch of SAI and once we are granted this divine touch that our life is filled with a new, rare, amazing spiritual joy. So come one, come all—devotees, seekers, come to Shirdi and attain the identity, the company, the love, the Kripa Prasad, that is, the grace of your Guru God Sai.

So be it! Om Sai Ram!

Nanda Deep

The divinity of the Lord is reflected in the Nanda Deep, the light generated from here illuminates our spiritual path—it feels as though the Lord Himself has merged as light in the illumination of the Nanda Deep. We have to make this visible light a means, along with the constant chanting of the Lord's name, devotion, love to attain the true light within. With these thresholds we have to keep holding onto the guiding light, we have to move on the spiritual path, ultimately illuminating or finding this outer light inside us; this light is ever-illuminative inside us but is lost in the mire of Maya. Ultimately our inner illumination should spread all around, as it becomes the basis of our life which ultimately merges into the Lord—the source of all light in this entire creation, so that we too illuminate with the self-illuminative Lord, that is, we are one with the Lord. Amid the darkness of Maya we have to get light from the Nanda Deep, so that we too move towards the permanent inner illumination, hence attaining the Lord, becoming one with Him, who is light Himself. Once we merge into the Lord, we too are ever-illuminative, divine.

While Baba lived in Shirdi bodily, He used to light diyas every evening at Nanda Deep, as though pouring His Divine messages through the light of the diyas lighted by Him. Firstly see your life as the diya. In this body, which represents a diya, arrange the wick of devotion drenched in the oil of love and surrender; light it with the spark of the Lord's grace, so that the light of Lord Sai illuminates your life. Even if there is darkness under this very light, don't let this light flicker or go off, as when the light of devotion, love, spirituality glows in your life only then will the darkness in your life, that is, Maya, be bound under this pious light. The light of spirituality alone can completely remove the darkness of Maya from our life, gather and bind it under its divine light. Before it is too late, trim the wick of devotion, love and surrender in your life in such a way that the Lord's grace illuminates it instantaneously with His Divine touch and this Divine light that is inherent in us, illuminates within us and is visible, can be seen and felt by us, more obviously.

By lighting diyas at Nanda Deep every evening, Baba also conveyed that if you have been given this precious human life, do not let it go waste—achieve and attain the true aim of your life—the Lord, the Light itself. Before old age knocks at your door, try to attain the Lord and be illuminated after being one with Him. Fill your mortal being with the Lord's name, His devotion and love to such an extent that before shedding the mortal coil, before the last lapse of your life, while still in the mortal coil, you attain the Lord of this body, achieve the very source of light, so that you too are illuminated because of and as that divine light.

Near the Nanda Deep there is a well where Baba had spread out His intestines to dry, that is, the inner self of the incarnated Lord had also presented itself for our benefit, for our upliftment. That divine self was seen radiating its Divinity and probably to salute this divinity, to salute this divine light with an outward light, that is, diya, Baba used to light diyas at the Nanda Deep.

Lighting a diya in the evening may have another meaning too—at the time of sunset the Lord Himself lighted the diyas probably to show the right direction to us foolish mortals and to make us feel secure. He felt that maybe after sunset, in the darkness of the night or Maya, His devotees, His lovely children might lose their right path in life. We mortals should recognise the true direction of our life with the light of this lamp and move towards the source of light, ultimately becoming light—the Lord himself.

It has been said that we generally have a companion who guides us on the right path, a mother's love nurtures the seed of life in her child, from a child to an adult, a Guru's grace bursts as knowledge for us, to make us reach our true destination, to put us on the path of deliverance and to merge us into the Lord. For use to be able to achieve the same, God Himself incarnates on this earth as a mortal being. By Himself lighting lamps, He gives a message of light to us mortals. He gives us a true feel of this Divine Ray of Light, and by making this ray of light the basis, a fortunate devotee attains the true Divine Light, that is, the devotee becomes light himself, hence bathing in the divine joy of deliverance. In the absence of such rare fortune, we mortals only search for Maya in the darkness under the light as we are basically attracted by darkness, bound by Maya. Even though being so close to the Light, we are foolishly lost in darkness, hence, embracing this darkness for digression on the path of life. Light is our inherent self but due to the dark veil of Maya this light is lost; we are unable to see the light though it is ever-illuminative inside us. To give us a feel of this true light and to highlight the Divine light inside us, Baba used to light lamps. By lighting the lamps outside Baba showed us the path that would enable us to gather the darkness of Maya and offering it to the darkness under the light we are able to reach the light within. We bathe in the Divine light of the Lord and are illuminated as the source of Light itself.

The light of Nanda Deep is telling us that the devotee who has attained the Lord's grace, he has been illuminated as the Lord Himself but the ones who dwell on ego, Maya, cleverness, cheating, hypocrisy, they only get the darkness under the light. Such a one can never attain light as it is darkness alone that pleases him. So that is what his fate was—darkness, Maya.

Try to understand, recognise and know the illuminative feel of the Lord from the light of the Nanda Deep. Fill this human life with the oil of love, devotion and surrender in such a way that the wick of spirituality instantaneously gets illuminated and its light fully fills our life in such a way that the devotee loses his or her identity and is merely a reflection of God. Breaking the shackles of Maya, he bathes in the Godly, divine and illuminative peace giving light of the Lord. He too illuminates as this light alone. We shed off the feel of I am a body; leave the tight grip of Maya and rejoice in the unification of the soul and the supersoul, where the devotee attains his Lord and is one with the Lord. Only light remains and nothing else, all darkness is wiped away or shed off, Maya is left far behind. Only the param tattva shines and it is this Divine Light that is in and around us, all over, always.

Amni's One Rupee

Baba's Dwarkamaayi is amazing, different, one of its own kind, from where our mother—Sai maa is always granting us love and protection. The place for each child is secure, assured in the lap of this Divine Mother. It is us mortals, who, in our Karmic cycle of give and take, in the engulfment of Maya are unable to understand, gather and feel this invisible security, the touch of the unseen love; God is a feeling—a wonderful feeling, to be felt by each one, individually.

The way Baba sat in the Dwarkamaayi for His children is actually a visible feel of His love and security granted to His children. His left leg is spread out to make His children sit on it, to give the joy of a mother's love, to shower selfless love on the heads that bow to this Divine mother—it feels and seems as though our mother has spread or outstretched a part of Herself, calling Her children to come and feel the 'embrace of Her unparalleled love.' Perpendicular to the left leg, the right leg that stands vertically straight, as though giving support or security to the left leg. Our Sai Maa has laid out Herself in the Dwarkamaayi to shower love on Her Children, to take them in Her protective embrace and yet, at the same time she is standing forever vigilant to provide protection to the dedicated children who have fully surrendered their all to Her. Our mother is constantly pouring love and protection on us but it is we children who are unable to gather this flow of spirituality even after placing our heads in Her lap, because our attention is always unfortunately focused on the by-products of Maya, that is, the ego, mine, *mayavi* (based on Maya) attractions and it is only in Maya that we rest. Someone wants material goods, someone else has greed for money, another desires name and fame, and yet another wants to experience the pleasure of a child. Countless children, each has his or her own way of thinking and each one has one's own capacity and capability to gather the Lord's grace. Only a rare one, a dear child, the one who has fully surrendered himself or herself at the mother's Lotus feet with a selfless self, can attain Sai Maa's grace through His loving protection and hence merge in the mother's lap and attain one's true mission in life—the Lord.

While Baba was present in a mortal coil, many children sat and played in His lap, received His loving touch and the divine joy of His being with them was not comparable to any other joy. That joy, the touch of a mother's love, the devotees experience even today in the pious lap of the Dwarkamaayi. One such fortunate child was Amni (Jamli's daughter) who had the good fortune of sitting in Baba's lap. Every day she would go to Baba to be blessed with the good and rare fortune of sitting in the lap of the Lord Himself. She would carry a small empty box with her with a desire that Baba would put a one rupee coin in her box, which Baba used to always give her, after showering a lot of love on her and as soon as she achieved her goal of getting the coin she world leave His lap and run away. Her mother would send her to Baba every day with clear and firm instructions that she should not leave Baba's lap till He gave her the one rupee coin.

This one rupee coin shows and teaches us the two sides of life—one side is the firmness of attaining one's mission and on the other side it brings to light the hunger for Maya. First face is firmness of mission and here Amni is the devotee whose sole mission is to get the one rupee coin and to achieve the same she is constantly encouraged by her mother—a mother is the first Guru for her child—the one who encourages us to be always focused on our aim and never lets us forget our true aim, till her child sits in the lap of the Guru maa, the Lord Himself and under His Divine protection, with His loving touch, bathing in the joy of His touch and by His grace alone attains or achieves the coin, that is, realises the true self—the Lord.

Baba gave a one rupee coin to Amni every day— neither two nor four as anything other than one portrays differentiation, that is, *dwaitya* (duality) and hence we are confused with this dual effect of Maya that places us in duality of everything; this duality gives us a feel of us being separate from the Lord, that is, we lose the feeling of oneness. Using one as a medium, Baba wants to give us a feel of *adwaitya* (one)—a feeling of non-duality that each one of us has to attain and achieve. We are born in dwaitya and though we grow in the same, we have to attain adwaitya under the protection of the Guru. We have to understand and feel this fact of life and imbibe it in each pore of our life that we, the Lord and all other beings are 'one'. We have to understand this reality and take this adwaitya as our true identity, hence shedding off dwaitya.

When we are born, duality becomes our basic nature but our true identity is a feel of oneness, which we have to attain by making use of the very cause of duality, this human form. The effect of Maya and its horrendous off-shoots are so powerful that even in an attempt to attain a feel of being one we are over and over again thrown into the mire of duality. The effect of Maya hinders us from being able to understand and achieve the feel of being one. It always dissuades us in a feel of mine and yours, which is duality. Probably that is why Baba made Amni a means to teach each one of us the lesson of oneness. He was actually explaining us the meaning of this entire creation being one, hence showing us the direction of *Sabka Malik Ek*. O Mortal being, though born in a feel of duality, you have to attain the truth of the soul, that is, the

Lord. Even while dwelling in this body, by recognising the oneness of all souls, you have to finally merge into your source, your base, the indivisible, omnipresent, omnipotent Lord Himself.

Om Sai Ram!

The other side that God probably wanted to show us is that we mortals are badly crushed under the burden created by the horrendous effect of Maya. Our unlimited desire to gather Maya and only want and aim for the same, that even after being blessed by the rare fortune of getting a human birth and getting the loving touch, divine joy of sitting in the Lord's lap we are unable to understand, know, gather the same, to be able to fully merge in the same because here too the slave at the Lord's feet, that is, Maya torments us. We find joy in the jingling of coins. The Lord tries His best to empty our box of life with His grace by throwing out materialism from it so that we are able to fill the same with our true identity—the Lord's light. But we, even while sitting on the origin of light, that is, in Sai's lap we desire Maya or darkness. Why do our ears yearn to hear the jingling sound of coins in our box of life? We give up light itself as we are deluded by the jingling of coins, hence the darkness—Maya. After aimlessly moving in this world of names and forms when we once again get place in the Lord's lap, then due to our unripe nature, we once again find ourselves entangled in the web of Maya.

The sound of the one rupee coin in Amni's box is a reminder for all of us to realise the hollowness of Maya by the jingling sound it makes, and this sound is singing the song for us to shed off duality and to adorn non-duality. Know the message hidden in this one rupee coin, the coin that has come from the Lord's Hand itself, carrying His Divine Message—We have to shed off duality to attain non-duality and while sitting in the protective lap of our mother Sai, we have to move on the path of spirituality, to embrace deliverance, hence leaving or shedding the desire for Maya in the lap of Mayapati, Sai, losing ourselves in a sense and feeling of non-duality. We have to achieve the true mission of our life in the loving embrace of our loving mother—Sai Maa. We have to rise above the darkness, leaving it there in His lap to attain light and to merge in the same. Here Amni is a means to introduce all of us to this hidden Divine fact. Baba used to make different devotees a means to make His divine messages reach one and all, and He is still doing the same. We all are only means to accomplish His divine tasks as He alone is the creator, the doer, the enjoyer and the wire puller. He alone showers His grace on His smaller parts to uplift them, to reach Him—their true Divine Self.

True Richness or Lordship is Hidden in *Fakiri*

Baba used to say that "true Lordship is hidden in *fakiri* (mendicancy)". Richness in terms of Maya, kingship of coins will vanish one day, we will never be able to gather it to the fullest as it is transitory by nature; it cannot stay permanently at one place. It is this Maya that gives birth to our ego but is unable to bear the weight of the ego for too long and so it just slips away quietly from the hands of an egoist. The foolish egoist is just left with his bloated ego and nothing else.

Each word uttered by Baba veils a deeper message for us and this fact that mendicancy is the real Lordship puts light on a hidden veiled, deep reality. Let us try to understand the same with Baba's permission and with His grace.

This mortal coil is a creation of Maya, it is fully dependant on Maya, it progresses on the path of life depending upon Maya and ultimately it is lost back or merges into Maya. This body is bound with the binding of birth and death while the Lord's identity, that is, the soul enters this mortal coil as its life to make it alive, it grants an opportunity to this lifeless body to be alive as the soul is ever free, unborn, indivisible the very basis of life.

The aim of human life is to achieve the unborn while being bound to the parameters of the one that is born, the body. We have to recognise the soul while bound to the body but we mortals are totally deluded by the irresistible attraction of Maya, bound to the limits of this body, hence we mortals are stuck to Maya only. We only nurture the comforts that progress this body hence entangling ourselves in the give and take of the Karmic cycle, as a result, forgetting or overlooking our true mission, that is, deliverance. We are unable to even get a feel of the soul within, leave alone achieving the same.

The one who is untouched or unaffected by Maya even while being amid Maya, even if surrounded fully by Maya and yet its touch does not waver that pious one, such a one is a *fakir* (mendicant). It is stated that a mendicant is fully drenched with the Lord's grace as the greed of Maya cannot even touch them; the effect of Maya cannot bind them fully. While in a mortal coil Maya does trouble them, whether fakir or saint, but they can put to rest the greed for the same by chanting the Lord's name, by devotion towards the Lord and by fully merging their life in the Lord's devotion, a point beyond our imagination. The mendicant who came to earth for the upliftment of humanity and through His own deeds, by His love towards the Lord, His devotional and unparalleled love for His devotees, He gave us a clear message that how, while dwelling in this mortal coil bound by Maya, in the midst of Maya, we can be unruffled by Maya by creating a protective shield of the Lord's name around us and by making His grace as the basis of our life, because He alone is the doer, we only enact His orders, the incarnated form of Lord—Sai Baba.

The Lord Himself in the guise of a mendicant, bound to a mortal coil kept showering the extraordinary divine nectar through ordinary bodily acts, that is, leelas. As a fakir, present in front of us in a form, in His own silent language He kept telling us that mendicancy is the real Lordship.

Let us try to understand and see this reality by opening our outer and inner eyes that what is the difference in the Lordship that Baba is talking about and what is the Lordship that we mortals are able to comprehend. For we mortals the true Lordship is the warmth of Maya, the jingling of coins, the glitter of gold, a desire to spread one's own name, a passion, a struggle to be the best as we are bound within the parameters of unlimited greed. What should we poor mortals do? Because, even this world bows in front of name and fame; everyone starts running behind the ones running for fame, name; in fact, behind innumerable people who are only running for money. We totally forget that the rat race for money has no true destination and greed, desires only fan the race for Maya with every passing life. When we bow our head in front of the Lord, it always carries some desire hidden inside, to be fulfilled, usually materialistic desires. Even while standing in front of the Lord we are unable to ask for the Lord as we are always yearning for Maya hence we only ask for and gather Maya and are always lost in the same. We mortal beings are bound to the mayavi richness because we only desire and gather Maya; we have not been able to even understand what fakiri is. Then how can we gather the true richness that is hidden in fakiri? We have not been able to even recognise it.

Where Maya dominates it's the richness of coins that remains, there Lakshmi is seated but God cannot be bound in the parameters of Lakshmi or Maya, so on the arrival of Lakshmi the Lord's light, the true identity of the soul is covered by the glitter of Maya, that only deludes. On the other hand where simplicity dwells, a state of fakiri predominates; there is no attachment, no greed for Maya. Where purity dwells, the Lord's name is active; where a desire to attain the Lord is pivotal, where there is madness of love to lose one's identity into that of the Lord, there the outer glitter has no significance. The acts that originate, stay, dwell and merge into Maya are irrelevant. Baba too used to get angry with people getting expensive gifts. Here it's only the inner feelings that are seen; love is at its apex. The Lord's identity is the most important mission of our life and hence ultimately that alone is unfurled. The veil of Maya is slowly removed and the light within illuminates. From the worldly eye we may look like a fakir. We may not have too much Maya or money, but the Lord's true identity starts resounding in each pore of our body and, the passion to achieve the Lord, to always be with Him grants us His True Divine Self.

Lord Himself resides in fakiri while in richness only the Lord's slave, Maya is seen. Now it is for each one of us to decide what really is true richness — Lord or Maya? Is it fakiri or the artificial adornment of Maya that has engulfed this entire creation, hence baffling one and all? Definitely fakiri. The Lord is our true asset, the richness that never leaves us. But the richness of Maya is transitory; it just slips away. The Lord is not transitory. He is firm and always present with us; in His unending Divine form, He is with His devotees, life after life, to ferry us across the sea of mundane existence.

Be fully drenched in the Lord's love to cross the ocean of mundane existence, by the guiding divine light of the Lord that is ever present in fakiri, hence shedding off greed, bondages and a want for the false richness that surely grants you outer glitter but makes your inner self hollow, hence giving you a feel of poverty, inner poverty.

What is the use of incomplete or unsatisfying richness? What is the use of the hollow outer glow? The glitter, the glow that is limited to only this life. Make the most of this mortal coil and fill your inner self with Godly radiance, the true richness. Let the outward attire be that of a fakir to be the true recipient of the the real richness, the attainer of the Lord's light, hence making this life worthwhile. Fill your human coil not with outer glitter but the glow of the soul, shed off the ornaments of gold and silver and wear the adornment of the Lord's name, glitter with the Divine Glow of the Lord in such a way that you are called the richest, the one who radiates the glitter of this rare gold—God. Baba has rightly said: "True richness or Lordship is hidden in fakiri".

Samadhi Mandir

(Form of Lakshmi–Narayan)

Lakshmi–Narayan are the basis of this entire creation. Seated on the Ksheer Sagar, sitting on the Shesh naag with its hoods as the umbrella, the creator of the entire creation and the very basis of the *dhwani* (sound)—Om are the reality of our life. Narayan is smiling with Lakshmi ji seated at His feet—this is the reality of our life; this is the basis of our life and it's from here that the seed of life has originated.

Our mortal coil has been created with the unification of five basics of life and due to the ingredient of material things this body is a representation of materialism only, may be that is why we mortals are always lost in Maya, ever rapt in it as we are created from Maya, but this mortal coil is useless, lifeless, unless a part of the Lord Himself enters this coil, as the soul, hence giving life to a lifeless form. This body is a combination, a coming together of the soul and Maya, so we see Narayan as the soul and Lakshmi or Maya as the body.

When Lakshmi–Narayan both are the basis to form this mortal coil that is why it is evident that the Omkar or Om sound originating from the Ksheer Sagar is always inside us. Though both are united but we can only see the body or the outer mayavi form; it's the joys and sorrows of this coil that pave our life and that is why all that gives comfort is dear to all of us. We humans are lost only in a bodily self; we adorn the confusion of our Karmic cycle by fully giving ourselves to the outer artificial self, though it is the soul that really is more meaningful, the very basis of life. It is the representation of God inside us; the soul that cannot be seen, but can only be felt. For this we will have to make an effort to give up the feel of the bodily self, while in this body, we will have to give up the attractions and wants of this body to the vast sea—Sai.

We humans are really caught up bodily; what is visible is an illusion of Maya, that is not going to last for very long—a reason for joy and sorrow in our life. On the other hand that which we cannot see and is merely a feel and an experience, the one that puts life into Maya, the one that is right in the midst of Maya yet not entangled by it, that is our true identity—our soul; that is the true form of the Lord, a part of the Lord Himself, our true identity. So make this mortal coil a means to reach, understand and achieve the true self—to generate and hear the Om sound resounding inside us, so that we can easily cross the ocean of mundane existence.

To make us understand, to instil in us over and over again that Lakshmi and Narayan are always together, they cannot be separated, as their being together is natural, as the true living example of the same is our body—there is no doubt about this fact. Each mortal coil portrays the unification of Lakshmi and Narayan, but we mortals forget Narayan, we lose ourselves in the glitter of Lakshmi or Maya, hence we keep spinning in a cycle of birth–rebirth.

Baba's Samadhi Mandir, even today introduces us to this fact. He is practically showing us that Narayan is surrounded by Lakshmi yet this Maya or Lakshmi is not able to touch Narayan. Even after, apparently engulfing Narayan, Lakshmi is not able to embrace Narayan. As Lakshmi will be lost in the flow of life, it will merge into the five elements of nature, but Narayan, the soul, is unending and will keep playing with Lakshmi over and over again, finding place in one form or another.

As a diamond is nicely arranged in gold, similarly the amazing, unique, unparalleled, ever-alive, indivisible jewel, that is, Narayan has been nicely, fully placed amid gold or Maya in the Samadhi Mandir in Shirdi. Today Baba is surrounded on all sides by gold as this form of Maya pleases the mortal being of this Kalyug, while actually we have to attain that 'unique diamond', by making gold or this body a means. We have to achieve the diamond embedded in this gold. The rare priceless diamond or Sai has been fully embedded in gold. Gold is only an outer form; we have to attain the amazing, unique divine diamond that is only radiating divinity. We have to lose ourselves in its glitter and unparalleled divinity.

Today's Samadhi Mandir portrays the divinely seated Narayan on the Ksheer Sagar. Here Narayan, seated in the middle of Maya, pleases one and all. Many devotees come to get a glimpse of the Lord, but due to the effect of Kalyug they admire the glitter of Maya and move ahead, while what we have to attain is Narayan, seated amid the glitter of Maya. We have to cross the illusion of Maya, the glitter of gold and worship only Narayan, hence admiring, attaining the same and finally merging into our origin, Narayan. We have to lose our identity in the divine light of the Lord. This is the fact that Sai Baba is telling us practically in the Samadhi Mandir. By sitting right in the centre of Maya, Narayan is guiding us to our true reality.

It is very difficult for us mortals to cross the threshold of Maya, attraction for gold and get over the greed for the same as we are born from Maya, we live on greed for the same and ultimately are lost into Maya. Hence, we are unable to cross or get over the greed, desire and attraction of gold or Maya. Our senses and desires, glitter of Maya, ever keep us blinded and hence we keep going deeper into the horrendous mire of Maya; we lose ourselves to its deceptive form and forget to cross the threshold of Maya.

Today, in the Samadhi Mandir Narayan Sai, seated amid Maya is calling us with open arms, as though inspiring us by His words, "O mortal being! Keep moving on, depending fully on my name, faith in my name and love, by shedding off the comfort of the senses and by leaving aside the delusion of Maya. Cross the threshold of mundane existence, to ultimately merge in me." Is it that simple? As we mortals are fully enslaved by Maya, our mortal coil too has originated from Maya.

If we have firm faith, consorts of faith and patience adorn us and we are constantly chanting the Lord's name with every breath then the force of Maya slowly keeps waning. We see or perceive gold as only a shining object—it does not blind our eyes, mind or intentions. Slowly, with the passage of time, the Lord's name, faith in His name and unconditional love towards Him bears fruit and the glitter of gold diminishes or is lost in the divine, undivided light of the Lord. When the glitter of gold becomes incompetent in blinding us, that we will be able to see and progress on the path of spirituality with a clear vision, to ultimately reach the divine Light—Narayan. This will happen once we cross the artificial, transitory, blinding glow of Maya.

We all want to merge in the divine glow of the Lord, we want to attain that rare jewel—Narayan—but He is seated in the centre of Maya. He has bound Himself and His Samadhi in the glitter of gold, sitting there and smiling. How should we reach Him? How should we be one with Him? How should we cross the threshold of Maya? How should we cross the glitter of gold to attain the path of salvation? Baba has practically shown us the reply to this question too, in the Samadhi Mandir. He has shown us the path to reach Narayan, even though, He is seated amid Maya. To get an embrace of the Lord, to merge the soul in the pious Samadhi, even today the three steps reaching or leading us to the Samadhi are free from the effects of Maya, even though Maya has fully surrounded Narayan from all sides, but it is incapable

Samadhi Mandir (Form of Lakshmi–Narayan)

to conceal His Divinity; Maya can surround but not hinder or overpower the Divine glow—Narayan.

Baba is trying to instil in us, over and over again that, "O mortal being, you can attain Narayan even amid Maya; by crossing the Kalyugi effect of Maya, you can merge in me—by moving on the path of spirituality, by crossing the three steps that will directly get you to me, by treading the path that takes the devotee straight to God, beyond the shore of mundane existence by the power of my name, on the spiritual path when a devotee is not affected by Maya, even while living in Maya." We are not deluded by the glitter of Maya even being amid the same.

The task assigned to our eyes is vision, that is to see, so look at Maya, that is, gold it is beautiful, appreciate the same (let the senses do their work, as Baba has said in the *Sai Sat Charita*) but don't let the senses be deluded by this delusion of Maya as it is only an outward attraction, which looks beautiful but is fatal—this is Maya. Keep yourself focused on the rare diamond (Baba) who is showing you the path of deliverance even amid Maya (cross the threshold of mundane existence with and in Maya yet to go beyond Maya). Climb the three steps made of devotion, love and surrender at His Lotus feet (not physically), move ahead, as only this path is clear and clean. Maya has no effect on love, devotion and surrender. Tread this spiritual path based on love, devotion and surrender to adorn the ornaments of devotion and patience, and fill the self with the Lord's name. Then you are sure to attain the Lord in this very life. After gaining and gathering the Lord's Divine Bliss we mortals (born of Maya) are able to break the web of Maya, to reach the Lord of Maya—Narayan.

Gold signifies Lakshmi or Maya, and Baba is Narayan. It is a known fact that Lakshmi follows Narayan as even on the Ksheer Sagar the Lord is seated with Lakshmi ji at His Lotus feet, both Lakshmi and Narayan are radiating the pious sound of Om. Lakshmi is nothing but the visible form of the Lord Himself. So amid His visible form, by making this form a means, we have to attain Her master, that is, Narayan. In front of her, we have to embrace deliverance by merging into the Lord; we have to shed off the means and attain our goal—the aim of life. We have to shed off Maya and lose ourself in the identity of our aim—Narayan or Sai.

Go to the Samadhi Mandir, in that pure atmosphere that is fully saturated with the Lord's name; awaken your inner self to the sound of His pious name, look at the gold or Maya surrounding Him, appreciate it, but only admire the Lord amid the pious flow of His name. Assimilate only the master of Maya—Sai—who is seated amid Maya but is totally unaffected, untouched by it. Try to understand that the glow falling on the paleness, yellowness of gold is the pious, white divine glow of the Lord. It's the glow of the Lord that is cleaning, cleansing the yellowness of gold to give it its divine glitter. Then slowly with devotional love devoid of Maya and full of surrender and dedication, cross the three steps, that is, childhood, youth, old age—complete life; or Rajas, Sattva, Tamas, that is, bearing the three gunas and attain the rare, indivisible, divine, ever-illuminating diamond—Lord Sai the God Himself. Achieve your true identity in His divine identity, losing yourself to a feel of Shivo Ham; be a recipient of deliverance, merging the flow of this river in the sea, lose your identity to be one with Him.

Shed off Maya, your identity with your body, to be who you really are—your true identity, your actual self, your real form—Sai.

Om Sai Ram!

(Samadhi Mandir conceals many more realities of the Lord. Here an attempt has been made to bring to light just one of them.)

Touch of the Samadhi, Joy of the Pothi (*Sai Sat Charita*) and Udi, Solution to all Problems

Incarnation of Lord Dattatreya, Sai Baba, came to Shirdi as a Saint, for the upliftment of His devotees, played innumerable leelas, as an offshoot of a simple straight life, the Leeladhar, Sai granted humanity its true identity at every step of life. He granted us the good fortune of His divine company at every step of our life, in each action, every deed, in His own different, divine way, teaching us something new at each step. He created His *avatar* (being) in such a way that, if we mortals gathered His grace every moment, every minute, with every breath, it would still be unimaginable for us and beyond our perception.

Whatever leelas He created, whatever grace He showered on us, while being in a mortal coil, they were our guide on the path of spirituality. His leelas alone came to us as His Voice, to enhance us on the path of love and devotion. It is impossible to gather them or count them all, as there is no end to His leelas—such as the vast endless sea.

After shedding His mortal coil, even today Baba is with us in His infinite formless self but we mortals, due to the bondages of this mortal coil, are not well equipped to gather His endless or concealed infinite self because we take Maya as our reality. We only take those facts as reality that we can see, listen or touch. The reality of experience is only highlighted once we have gathered the reality, that is God by touch, as a visible reality by looking at His physical form and that's what actually pleases us, because we too are in a physical form. That is why even after shedding off His mortal coil Baba granted us His live form, which is a means for us to reach the unending omnipresent form of the Lord, hence attaining the formless reality of the Lord, not visible to the human eye. Baba showed us the path of the three steps that lead us to the Dwarkamaayi or His Samadhi in the Samadhi Mandir; Baba granted us three possessions which are a means to reach His infinite, true self. We càn merge into the pure chaitanya by crossing these three steps, hence becoming the light itself, to bathe in His divine joy. The three steps, His three possessions that He granted us as boons are—the touch of the Samadhi, joy of the pothi (*Sai Sat Charita*), and a path to attain solutions to all problems that is hidden in His Udi.

The Lord incarnated on the earth as a saint and made Shirdi His Karma Bhoomi. He performed the deeds, of a simple ideal life, the colour of these deeds being called His leelas, hence showing, we mortals, the path of honesty, simplicity, goodness, that is, the path of spirituality. He granted the touch of the Lord, His divine joy, unparalleled elation, by binding Himself in the boundaries of the body. He showered divinity on us even though bound to a mortal coil, even after adorning the guise of a fakir. He showered love and spirituality—the true riches of the Lord on us. He crowned us with endless grace even though He was bound to the boundaries of the mortal coil. An incarnation of Lord Dattatreya, Lord Sai incarnated as a saint for human upliftment by binding divinity or the Lord Himself in the parameters of the body and granted us the grace of His deeds in the form of amazing leelas—the leelas that are actually ideals for us—as the guide that led and are still leading us to the divine joy of the Lord. The leelas, though apparently simple, they act as a shower of the Lord's extraordinary grace in our life and give us a feel of the unparalleled light by drenching us with their Divine joy.

This mortal coil has been created to be lost one day; life is born to move towards its end, so the end of this mortal coil is assured. When we ordinary mortals leave this coil—then earth is lost to earth and the soul either attains deliverance, hence attaining the indivisible formless self of the Lord, or is re-born in a new mortal form. On the other hand when the Lord incarnates on this earth after the accomplishment of His incarnation then the incarnated form merges in the five elements of nature and the Lord, bound in the coil, is alive all around us in His formless, omnipresent indivisible form. His form is felt and seen in the smallest speck; He is highlighted in His formless self, that is, His unborn, ever-free and divine self that is an integral part of this entire creation. His omnipresence can be felt even after His incarnated form rests in the Samadhi as He is an integral and essential part of each mortal coil, each speck of this creation, every pore of this universe.

We mortals are slaves of this mortal coil and hence crave to get proofs for everything—we are bound to the sense of touch, whatever is visible to these eyes. We, at times, get a feel of this unseen reality of the Lord yet at other times we doubt the very being of that superpower. Unfortunately we are only able to know, recognise and understand those facts that we can see, touch or feel. For this very reason, even after leaving His mortal coil Baba left some possessions for us after His Mahasamadhi, which we can feel, see, touch and hence adorn the same to strengthen our faith. These three possessions are—

— Touch or feel of the Samadhi

— Joy of the pothi (*Sai Sat Charita*)

— Udi, the solution to all our problems

1. Touch or feel of the Samadhi

While Baba was in a mortal coil He had said, "Even after casting off this mortal coil, my Samadhi will talk to my devotees; it will move and will be ever eager for the upliftment of one and all." This fact that was uttered from Shriji's mouth can be felt and experienced by one and all, as even after His Mahasamadhi, His Samadhi absorbs all the difficulties of His devotees, that is why there is a never ending queue leading to the Samadhi Mandir to gather the pious, pure divine grace of the Lord; to get a glimpse of Lord Sai's Samadhi from where the Lord Himself is ever-alive. It is impossible to bind the radiance of the sun, it is not possible to engulf and gather the air, similarly it is not possible to bind the Lord's Divinity, uninterrupted self, His omnipresence. His divinity is radiating and emerging from His Samadhi even today. Even iron transforms into gold by the touch of *paras* (philosopher's stone). Similarly by getting a feel of the Lord's Samadhi, this mortal coil also transforms and glitters. Divinity is basically an essential and integral part of each one of us; all of a sudden it becomes clear and hence is clearly visible by His grace. This divine light enters our life enhancing us on the path of spirituality, putting, us mortals, on the path of the true mission of our life—deliverance. It is the touch of the Samadhi that Lord Sai has granted us for our transformation from iron to gold, it acts as paras, that is, amid this world it liberates us from our bodily self, granting us the joy of the soul. It gives us a glimpse of the concealed Godly light. It makes us a pure, pious recipient of being able to move on this path of spirituality—the 'touch of the Samadhi', that is, our 'Direct Connection' with the Lord. That divine touch which burns up all our misdeeds, washes away all ill in our life and introduces us to the Lord in such a way that the soul within us gets its true feel or true touch, bathes in aatmic elation, shedding off bodily off-shoots—sin, sorrow, misfortune, gets a glimpse of its true identity, that is, the soul and dances in joy as it gets the fortune of walking on the path that leads us to the Lord Almighty, that is, it gets the jewel of peace. So the touch of the Samadhi means our being 'face to face' with Baba—our divine connection with Him and ultimately our aatmic elation.

2. Secondly, Baba granted us joy of the pothi (*Sai Sat Charita*)

We only gain the joy of His grace from the pothi as Baba Himself had given adesh (permission) to Hemadpant to write the same—He had said, "Surrender at my feet by completely giving up your ego as I myself will describe my leelas, singing the song of my life, you being only an outward means. I will myself narrate my life story by entering your inner self." *Sai Sat Charita* was written by Baba Himself, making Hemadpant a means for the same and this is a proven fact that whatever the Lord grants us is a source of joy alone. Hence each letter of the *Sai Sat Charita* is 'pure nectar', and the Lord's love is flowing ceaselessly from the same. We have to gather the same with our devotion, surrender and faith to attain our own true selves in each alphabet of this 'pure Chaitanya'. After understanding and imbibing this reality we have to merge our entire self in this very reality.

The Lord's grace always flows to those who become means to write the life of saints, in fact it is His grace that makes it possible to write the granth. The same has been written in *Sai Sat Charita* also:

Sant Charita je je lihiti, Tayavari Bhagvantachi Preeti, Aiyse Maharaj Gyaneshwar Vaditi, Dharavi Bheeti Mag Mee Kaan

(Chapter 2, Ovi 17, *Shri Sai Sat Charita*)

Maharaj Gyaneshwar says, "Lord enters into a pure, fearless inner self, hence singing His own life story."

It is Baba's grace alone that innumerable devotees are able to read this pure, pious granth today. The Shirdi Sai Baba Sansthan has got this original marathi granth translated into many languages—each devotee cherishes the joy of the same in their own mother tongue, as the difference of language cannot bind the pure ambrosia flowing from the same—the nectar of the Lord's name, His leelas, His love, His grace. By His grace I too did parayan (a regular reading) of the same, many a times, at times in English and at other times in Hindi—undoubtedly gaining a rare pearl each time I dived into this vast ocean. With each reading this soul adorned a new, amazing, rare knowledge by the grace of God. For quite some time I was unaware that the basic Marathi granth has been written in *Ovi* form and that beyond the abridged version its flow is ceaseless, magnanimous. I had the first glimpse of the basic Marathi Granth in Baba's Dwarkamaayi—a desire to read the same arose in my mind and was fructified. Though I do not know Marathi yet Baba's grace granted me this basic Marathi pothi. Initially when I started reading the same, I could not go beyond 10–12 *ovis* a day. The first time I completed the same, Baba called me to Shirdi and granted me the darshan of Siddhi Vinayak and Gyaneshwar Maharaj, along with His own divine glimpse which was a reward for this soul. My mind was elated and I was once again eager to read the same and by His grace I am reading this Marathi pothi for the fifth time and it is His grace alone that is enabling me to read one chapter every day. Though I am not familiar with Marathi yet it seems as though a lot is being understood by me. While reading some ovis a very different feel fills me, as though Baba is saying, "Gather this particular pearl for today." So I, once again enjoy the same ovis, and it's His grace that enables me to understand its meaning to a large extent and the rest I ask from someone who knows Marathi, just to put a stamp on what I have understood by His grace. It feels as though the words read go straight and touch the depths of my soul, vibrating the strings of love within. I actually feel a different joy in reading the original Marathi pothi. As the light in the sun cannot be replaced by any number of candles or artificial lights and the original has actually been penned down by Baba. While we read the same, each one gathers something original according to one's thoughts, deeds and state of mind. Each one's level or threshold to understand, gather and assimilate the same is different. In the same way when the original is translated then the ambrosia remains unchanged but the thoughts, mental state and the ripeness to understand the same by the translators can be felt in the same. So when we read the 'original' we get an uninterrupted flow of Divinity which is flawless, without the shades and the feelings of the translator.

We read the Vishnu Sahstra Naam in Sanskrit though we might quench our thirst to understand the meaning in a simpler, familiar language but the chanting of the same in the original language purifies the atmosphere, the ears feel the flow of pure amrit through these words and the resounding of the thousand names of the Lord attains its Divine Place in our soul. Baba made Shama read Vishnu Sahastranaam though he never knew Sanskrit language yet he could bathe in the Ganges of the 1000 names of the Lord, in fact remember them by heart.

This does not mean that we should not read translated Granth. It is essential, as we can only adorn the original after understanding, assimilating the same in our own language. Just as we move from the manifest to the unmanifest form of the Lord, from known to the unknown but the base in both is God. In order to reach the crux, original just try to understand and know what is easily understood and then move towards the crux, the basis of the creation. Baba Himself will introduce you to His own self, unfurling His true self hidden in the basic. Each soul gathers, understands, imbibes the words uttered from the Lord's mouth according to each one's spiritual situation or enhancement, and so the sweetness of the *Sai Sat Charita* slowly keeps sinking inside each one of us. As we shed off the bitterness of our misdeeds that the basic unmanifest, the omnipresent form of the Lord will establish more obviously inside us. Each word of the *Sai Sat Charita* will pierce our body to give our soul a feel, a touch of the Lord, after worshipping the Lord in a form, we will be able to understand His unmanifest omnipresent self. Similarly after reading the pothi in our own language each word of the original pothi will establish itself within us, the name of the Lord will elate our inner self. We will reach a state:

Arimesh tujhe Nama Vartan, Henchi amha katha kirtan, Henchi amhyache Nitya anusandhan, Henchi Samadhan amhyache.

(Ovi 25, Chapter 26, *Shri Sai Sat Charita*)

Meaning—"Always chanting the name of the Lord is our *Katha Kirtan* (reading or singing His praise), and His name alone is the solution to all our problems." So chant the Lord's name always, and His name and His being are an integral part of each speck of the Universe, it is in each pore of our body, but to be able to know, understand and recognise His omnipresence take the aid of His manifest form and His name—make His name the aim of your life. His name is an integral part of each word in the pothi; bathe in this flow of bliss to merge into the same—Sai.

As we sing the *artis* (songs sung in the Lord's praise) in the language they are written in and after repeated singing they become an integral part of our system, similarly we can gather the pearls of knowledge from the basic original pothi by repeatedly listening and reading the same. The reading of this pious granth introduces us to our Guru God, plants the sapling of devotion in our hearts, bathes us in a flow of love and brings us face to face with the Lord, that is, our true self. That is why this pious Granth states—

**Gurusenesi je tatpar, Guruvagyecha jya adar,
Ishtanishtecha sarva Vichar, Gurushiravar to thenvi,
Guruyagecha to kinkar, Swatantra nahi tya Vichar,
Nitya Guru Vachan Palanpar, Sarasar dekhena**

(Ovi 141–142, Ch. 23, *Shri Sai Sat Charita*)

Meaning—One who is ever eager to serve the Guru, one who respects the Guru's words, surrendering all good and bad thoughts at His Lotus feet, who adheres to and follows the Guru's words, who has no independent thoughts of his own and who follows the Guru's words alone, he has seen or understood this world in the true sense.

Such a dedicated one can gather the Lord and is capable of creating or writing a Saint's life, as the Guru's grace finds its seat in such a selfless inner self, free of ego on the threshold of complete surrender and this grace ferries a devotee to unknown, unseen and unimagined shores. The best, joyous step that leads us to our Guru is the pothi. Read it regularly till each word fills each and every pore of your body, then, with time its divine words will automatically radiate from within and the melody playing "Sai, Sai, Sai", His divine identity, will flow from within. God will surely Grant us this state one day.

**Chitta Sai Naam Smarni
Drishti Sai Samarth Charni
Vritti Sai Dhyan Dharni
Dehkarni Saichya**

(Ch. 23, Ovi. 143, *Shri Sai Sat Charita*)

Meaning—"A state when the inner self will always meditate on Sai, the eyes will be stuck at His Lotus feet. Our entire vision will be rapt in Sai's form, and this body will be only a reason, a means to spread His name."

We will bathe in the bliss of the soul, while being tied to the parameters of the body, even though we are ignorant beings yet the joy of the original pothi, the hidden touch of the Lord in the same will bathe us in its flow of nectar. Sai Baba Himself will feed us with the nectar of each word of the pothi. *Animesh* (meaning in Marathi—all the time)—all the time, in His own deep yet subtle way He will grant us Shri from each speck of the pothi, that is, He will show us the Lord God in each word of the pothi. Maybe then one day this body will be able to read this pious granth in seven days, that is, do the parayan and will take the fruit of the Lord's grace as its best fortune imbibing it in each pore of the body to attain unparalleled joy in this life itself.

As sight fructifies the very being of eyes, voice is the identification of the throat, the glow of knowledge removes the darkness of ignorance, the feel, the touch of the soul liberates us from our bodily self, love of the Gopis alone feeds Lord Krishna with makhan, the flow of cool breeze removes the scorching heat, the touch of water droplets quenches the dryness of the soil, similarly each word of the Lord's life written by the Lord Himself fructifies human life on earth, grants us our true identity, fills our inner self with the joy of the Lord's name so that our life always bathes in this joy. Just like the pious flow of the river Ganges, while reading the original pothi, we merge into the Lord who is an integral part of His own life, and attain our true identity. As it is essential to breathe in order to stay alive, similarly make the life of Saints an integral essential part of your life, read their marvels every day, then see how in this ignorant mortal coil, full of the darkness of Maya, the Lord's light will be seen. Even though a mortal being, you will merely be your Guru's reflection. By His grace you will be able to radiate His Divine light all around, after assimilating the same. This is the effect of the *Sai Sat Charita*. This is the effect of the pure ambrosia flowing from the pothi. Before this mortal coil ends its journey, make the most of it,, that is, a means to attain the Lord. Read the *Sai Sat Charita* daily, so that along with this outer coil, the inner self finds its true identity—merges into the Lord Almighty.

Om Sai Ram!

3. The third grace that Lord Sai has granted us is Udi, the solution to all our problems

The sacred ash that we get from the sacred fire in the Dwarkamaayi is called Udi. As per its face value it is mere ash but actually it is no less than *Sanjivani* (life-granting herb), in fact it is Sanjivani, which is a cure to all—for material and spiritual gains, for freedom from worries of the body and mind and Ram Baan for our spiritual progress. From Baba's Guru Sthaan, four diyas were found burning that signified Dharma, Artha, Kama and Moksha and that found a place in His Karma Bhoomi, that is, the Dwarkamaayi as the Dhuni Maai—the pious fire. Baba's *tapasya* (penance) shone as Dhooni and it is this ever-illuminative tapasya of the Lord God Himself that could quench the sorrow, sadness and pain of His devotees. Dhuni Maai accepts coconut, food, wood, etc., as our misdeeds, misfortunes and we offer them to put an end to these negativities, to burn them down and with an end to our sorrow and difficulties is born the *Vijay Pataka* (the flag of victory)—the Udi.

The tilak of Udi on our forehead is an open announcement and repeated reminder that—difficulties and sorrows have been burnt to ash; the pious fire of the Dhuni has put an end to them. Our journey to success, our spiritual path begins, once our sorrow and misfortunes have been put to rest or burnt down. The tilak of Udi on our forehead is an announcement that we have won over sorrow and that bodily tortures do not trouble us anymore. This tilak signifies the diminishing effect of bodily, material things and marks our accelerated growth on the spiritual path. This ash on our forehead is a reminder that one day our body too will be ash, so while alive, take this body to be nothing else but ash and try to know, gather and understand the Lord's reality concealed in this ash, that is in our body as the *atman* (soul). Fire cannot burn down this reality which is our true identity—the soul. This reality of life, our soul, will get face to face with the basis of our life, that is, Sai, the Lord Almighty, merging the soul into the supersoul.

Baba too used to say that Udi is a means to introduce you to the transitory nature of your body—this body is mortal and will be ash one day but the soul, which is a part of the supersoul, will merge into its identity when the body is lost or will be assigned a new form according to the good or bad deeds performed as the soul is unborn, untouched, ever free and yet binds itself to a form for its deliverance.

The mark of Udi on our forehead is our faith, that after burning all the bad, under the protection of the Lord we have got this victory mark, as a result of our Guru God Sai Baba's grace. This victory mark—Udi will give this body its own form, that is ash, one day, but till then don't let this body waver from the path of honesty, spirituality and love as this sacred mark on our forehead is a proof of our faith, which will ferry us from this mundane existence to give us peace in the safe lap of our Sai Maa.

While Baba bodily lived in Shirdi, He used to distribute Udi to one and all, as Prasad; Udi that quenched all our bodily, material sufferings, and even today it is our *Sanjivani* (life-giving herb) that grants us a good, spiritual, healthy life by uprooting our sorrows and pain by its amazing efficacy. It soaks all our misdeeds to grant us a clean, glittering, life devoid of ill thoughts. Udi is actually made from quite a few things put together, offered to fire as oblation and the remains of the same is Udi but its Godly, divine, amazing effect is not in the Udi but has its direct connection to Lord Sai. It's His grace that is showered on us through this Udi. If we have full faith in its efficacy the Godly grace hidden in the same is revealed. Udi is effective according to our faith in its efficacy. On the threshold of disbelief, for a doubting, unbelieving inner self, Udi is only ash. It's our faith that fills life into the same to make it Sanjivani. The touch of the Lord, His divine joy, the Udi grants us a solution for any and all problems, hence granting us the fruit of our faith and firm conviction in our Lord Sai. The Lotus of spirituality blossoms in our heart after soaking all bodily and material sufferings, that is, getting rid of them. Though in the form of ash, yet Udi is our saviour, repeatedly reminding us that this body is nothing but ash and that we will use this transitory body, which is nothing but ash to attain God, by having full faith in His grace and embracing self-realisation.

O mortals! Do not let time slip out of your hand, don't entangle yourself too much in desires or wants. Make Lord Sai Baba's name the basis of your life from today itself, get the pious feel of His Divine Samadhi in Shirdi. Read the pothi every day, savouring the flow of Godly joy from the same, and put the victory mark of Udi on your forehead every day as your faith, hence attaining a solution to all problems through this sacred ash. At every step of your life remember the pious touch or feel of the Samadhi, the live flow of spirituality; make the joy of the pothi a part of each incoming and outgoing breath; and fill your faith in the Udi, with the pious name of Sai; then surely your life will be fulfilling and will glitter with this Divine fulfilment. O mortal being, even while dwelling in this body you attain the unborn Lord Almighty and you will be standing at the door of deliverance, smiling with contentment.

Shri Sai leela Magazine, (Shirdi), March–April, 2009

Why did Baba Adorn the *Kafni*?

Mendicants have their own typical way of dress and adornment, whereby there are saintly saffron clothes to cover the mortal coil adorned by the saints. Mendicants are lost in their own world, wearing their own typical dress, covering themselves fully with the identity of God; they keep moving on the path of devotion, making their life a basis, a model, hence showing millions of people the path of love and devotion, they ferry them across.

Why did our Lord Sai adorn a Kafni in His saintly incarnation? We all know that initially Baba was seen in Shirdi as a wrestler, with His hair open. After losing a game of wrestling played with Mohiddin Tamboli, Baba changed His way of dressing and He started wearing a Kafni which was white in colour or sometimes even green in colour and wore his hair like a bun on the left side and tied it with a head gear. Why did Baba adorn such clothes?

This is a known fact that whatever Baba did concealed some deep reality within, a message for us to grasp and His adorning a Kafni and a *patka* (head gear) are no exception. Each one of us can interpret the same according to our own view point in the way that He wants us to, but the flow of thoughts that Baba showered on me, are being shared with one and all as His message.

Open hair and the adornment of a wrestler signify this human coil, whereby each one of us has learnt, are eager to execute the fact as that's what we have seen on this path of life—to be strongest of all. Darwin too propagated the fact of survival of the fittest in his theory of Evolution. This creation is such that the stronger wins over the weaker—from an ant to a bird or animals and ultimately us humans. Human tendency, especially in this Kalyug is fully standing on the platform of selfishness, me and mine. So this selfish tendency teaches us to gather for our own selves right from the inception of life. But we only want to gather everything at any cost, even if it means snatching from others, and this selfish tendency goes on increasing with our growing age. We learn the lesson of 'my benefit' very early in life, hence making it the very base or the basis of our life. When the base is on the threshold of selfishness then you can imagine the direction of our growth.

In the formative years of life we are like an open book or a *Tabula Raza* (clean slate). Whatever is inscribed on the same has a very deep effect on our life as that becomes the basis of our life. These tendencies are not essentially taught by our parents but the effect of their Karma that falls on us are their reflection. Now whether we build the castle of our life on the threshold of goodness or give way to evil deeds, depends on us to a large extent as well as on our deeds.

We are left in a wrestling rink of life at birth, whether we attain victory or defeat, yet we have to keep fighting to be victorious, always. A rare soul develops a sense of vairagya after losing in this wrestling rink of life, leading a spiritual life with honesty and satiation. Most of the time we keep fighting for victory and it becomes our sole mission. A rare one lives a devoted life full of love for the Lord, filled with His name, so that in this very life, while moving on the path of spirituality, such a one attains the true aim of life, merges into the Lord and embraces liberation.

The attire of a wrestler signifies that we can win in the rink of life only by force and open hair signifies that where force is the way of life, Maya is the basis of the lifestyle. There even our thoughts or our *buddhi* (intelligence) is similar to an open rink or open hair, that is, there is no control over one's thoughts. Hence Maya repeatedly strikes on these susceptible thought processes and the open hair, signifying a brain filled with Maya, is further entangled in its web by Maya. We humans, who are filled with Maya, encouraged or initiated by Maya keep fighting for Maya, life after life. We are entangled in the open jigsaw of our thoughts, based on greed for Maya, losing our own identity in the hands of Maya, and hence losing ourselves in fighting for Maya, all our lives. This does not mean that Baba was entangling Himself in Maya by keeping His hair open but was giving us this message that our life is full of Maya, hence it pushes us constantly in the rink of life, to only win. But the satiation one can attain in losing in this rink cannot be felt in a constant desire to win as here the defeat is of me, mine, and the ego and our true or real victory is hidden or concealed in this defeat. O Mortal being, the Lord or rather your life has placed you in this rink of life to attain the fruit of victory, in this rink created by Maya based on your deeds, and if you keep fighting and struggling for this outward victory then you will keep wandering from one rink to another from one life to another. On the other hand if you deeply understand the defeat of this body, deeply understand and realise this defeat as your true victory and move on in life, then you can surely attain the true aim of your life; you can attain God by moving on the path of spirituality as it is only when Maya is defeated that it can be suppressed and its artificial veil can be removed and it is here that the light of the Lord glows or illuminates the entire being.

Instead of letting this mortal coil fight constantly for material assets, lose yourself in the rink of this life, that is, give up me, mine your ego, so that you can move ahead on

Why did Baba Adorn the Kafni?

the spiritual path with a pious self after crossing or leaving behind material name and fame, material victory. You become worthy of treading the spiritual path, hence attaining the Divine Light of the Lord. This truth Baba displayed, practically, by merely changing His attire. He showed how a wrestler, a human being who is rapt in amassing Maya, who has been constantly fighting in the rink of life, loses one day and in this defeat is hidden the defeat of his me, mine, ego, showing him the path of his true victory—a path that is beyond victory or loss; one that is based on surrender and ferries us to our destination on the consorts of love, devotion, dedication, faith, where like Baba's patka, our thoughts and our understanding too are tied with the Lord's name and our full faith in His name, so that we can firmly move on the path of love and devotion. The wrestler in the rink of Maya is adorned with the Kafni of devotion after losing in this rink and the hair-bound patka tied on the head represents the firmness in faith. Now such a one lives on whatever he or she gets as *bhiksha* (donation) from different houses, that is, to be satisfied and satiated with whatever is gained or received as the Lord's grace. Baba Himself is the Lord of Maya, hence Maya can't even touch or bind Him, so these so called deeds or leelas that He played were for our benefit alone, to show us the path of devotion, faith, basically for our upliftment.

Why did He adorn a Kafni and a patka. In our lifetime whatever clothes we wear have knots, buttons, ribbons, elastic, etc., as a means to be tied to our body but a Kafni has no such knot to be tied, no interruptions just free flowing and flawless. The clothes we wear depict a sense of bondage, we mortals who are bound by our thoughts, relationships, experiences and by our deeds; but once we are liberated from bad, negative thoughts ahamkaar, bad intentions only then are we granted the Kafni of loving devotion, which is bondage free. Our mortal coil is still the same, but the bondages that Maya had created have been opened or cut down, so that spirituality can flow in our life, uninterrupted. At the same time our enlarged, open hair are like our jumbled thought processes that are now bound with the firmness of unshaken faith, in the form of the patka. Your buddhi that keeps your entire mortal self under its control has now been fully bound by faith in the Lord; now your thoughts, your basic central unit is under the control of your Lord Sai—your faith in Him, your love towards Him. Now it is under your Guru God's control in such a way that your life is filled, in the true sense, with complete flow of the Lord's love and devotion as now your life is full or saturated with the Lord's love alone, devotion and devotional love.

In a Nut Shell

1. Clothes of a wrestler or ordinary mortal beings—full of knots or twists and curves signifying bondage—the bondages that display our desires, ego, etc.

2. Not to tie our hair or to leave them open—In the rink of life when the mortal coil is ever ready to fight and win at any cost, at that point our intellect, our thought processes are difficult to bind and are not under our control. These thoughts are open like the open hair and are further getting entangled due to desires, ego and a wholesome effect of Maya. Our own thoughts are not under our control when Maya, desires, ego keep dancing their horrendous dance on our thought processes.

3. To lose in a bout of wrestling—This defeat is in fact our real or pivotal victory as here it's not a defeat of our life but it's our life that has defeated Maya, that is, me, mine, our desires, ego. The defeat that conceals the true victory in itself. After losing in the rink of Maya, our spiritual path opens, only a down-to-earth, egoless individual can move fast towards the Light of the Lord. Our pace becomes very slow when we are carrying the weight of our ego, our desires, as a result we can break down and succumb to our own ego and desires.

4. Change in attire—The souls treading the path of spirituality depict a different colour altogether, an amazing form, that is, some souls are granted the Kafni of spirituality. In the absence of bondages, typical to Maya, the Lord's love flows in our life without any interruptions, obstacles—slowly and steadily filling our lives with its Divine Light.

5. Patka tied on the head—Hair tied inside a patka depicts that once we start treading the path of spirituality, are rapt in the praise of the Lord then the very origin of our thoughts are bound by the Lord, with the Lord, in His safe, secure hands. Now, like the entangled loose hair, our thoughts and desires will no longer get entangled, as now they have been tied or controlled at the origin itself with love, grace of the Guru and firm faith. Now the loving grace of God has been definitely bound to us, so that on the path of life, after adorning the long robe of spirituality no knots or barriers slow down our speed. Now the Lord's Divine light easily flows into our life, filling our life fully with this Divinity. Hence we merge into this very Divine Light.

By merely playing a bout of wrestling and changing His outward attire Baba conveyed to one and all, that we have to liberate our life from the clutches of Maya and at the same time tie our thoughts, ideas and keep them under control instead of entangling them further, so that we can live a bondage-free life, where Maya cannot cause hindrances—our ideas, our thoughts should only be tied to the name, love of the Lord and unblemished faith in the Lord.

Our life is like a wire full of empty space for current to flow but the current will not pass or the circuit will not be complete till we switch on the button. Our mortal coil too is lifeless like this wire, and it's the Lord's name, His love that flows as current in our body and once the button of spirituality is switched 'on' after sinking or drowning our ego, desires in the ocean of life, it's only then that this current, as Lord, flows inside us, divinely, without any hindrance, in this body that the bulb of His Divine light, which was lying dormant inside us, illuminates with the departure of Maya and on the arrival of spirituality. The Lord's Light shines inside us, spreading all around, its pious Divine glow.

Om Sai Ram!

The Kafni probably points towards another reality. In Hinduism while performing the last rites of a person all knots are cut, open or broken, before giving the body its final rest on its pyre, in the fire. So probably, the Kafni also gives us an indication towards this reality that to achieve the Lord and to finally merge into His Divine Form, that is, in the form of fire, to lose our identity in His ever-illuminative divine self, before giving up the five senses to His divinity, that is, fire, we mortals have be free of all kind of bondages, as only a liberated or bondage-free being can merge into the Lord and can find refuge in the Divine ever-illuminative form of the Lord. The soul is ever free, unbound and unborn. So at the time of leaving the mortal coil, all knots are cut so that the soul is shown the path to take its basic, natural flight, adorned with clean, non-entangled clothes. This is a reality during the last rites but the one who, while alive, in this mortal coil, amid the Karmic cycle, doing one's deeds with full dedication is liberated from the bondage of life adorning a free-flowing Kafni of vairagya, such a one is sure to cross the ocean of mundane existence. This is what Baba probably taught us by adorning the Kafni. He made the outer paraphernalia, His leelas a reason for our internal take off, for our internal enhancement.

Some fortunate souls were granted a Kafni used by Baba, as this is how the master of this body, Sai showed us the clean, uninterrupted path to reach Him. By granting His Kafni to a few devotees probably Baba indicated that now Sai Himself was going to take them to new heights of spirituality by keeping their thought processes under His control and was going to get them face to face with their true identity—the Lord Almighty.

Why did Baba Adorn the Kafni?

No *vastra* (adornment) can bind Baba, neither the bondage of life and death, nor is He desirous of deliverance as He Himself is the unborn, ever-free, omnipresent, Lord Almighty. He did all this to plant a sapling of devotion in our hearts, to awaken the true devotional love lying dormant within, so that we move on the path that leads to Him; He held our hand to lead us to our true destination, to merge into His true identity and to make us embrace true devotion and ultimately Him—Sai.

I was, I am, I always will be...

The Lord is omnipresent, omnipotent, all pervasive, ever alive. He is an integral part of all animate and inanimate things; each atom in this Universe engulfs His ever-alive self. As we mortal beings are bound to a mortal coil, hence we are not able to understand, gather, assimilate the unseen, omnipresent self of the Lord. That is why the Lord manifests on this earth again and again, sometimes as Rama or Krishna, as Lord Dattatreya or Sai, to ferry the devotees beyond the ocean of mundane existence, to show the true path to sinners while He Himself in an incarnated form lives a model life and saves us from the clutches of Maya by giving us the examples from His ideal life. He would live a normal mortal life amid Maya yet would be never troubled or touched by Maya. In fact all the incarnations of God saved their devotees from Maya by making Maya itself a means, established Dharma by putting an end to evil at the hands of goodness.

God first creates, then plays with the creation by rediscovering His own self, the soul, with the help of His own self, the physical form. This entire creation is nothing but the Lord, yet we are unable to find Him or understand Him. He Himself creates this entire creation, then manifests in this creation as life and then He makes us mortals dance in the ups and downs of our own deeds, yet we are unable to 'see' Him; and when He does not want to play any longer, the play of Karmas amuse Him no longer, then He merges His own separated part, the soul into His divine self, that is, life itself.

We mortals live a life as though it's we who are the doers hence battling in the conceit of our own ego, in the process troubling other forms of the Lord. We fools would walk with our heads high, as though we are the best and that is the basic reason we keep entangling ourselves in the cycle of birth–rebirth. In the process we are unable to attain our true mission—the Lord.

The task of the mind is to get entangled in desires, the brain is there to think and keep worrying for small little things, eyes have been assigned the task to see, wind always keeps blowing, water gives us a cool feeling, similarly the basic function of this body is to perform deeds but the soul in this mortal coil is ever free which has adorned this mortal coil with the sole mission of its elation, to finally merge into the *Paramatman* (the Lord). So the basic aim of the soul is the supersoul, to merge into the same, and that is the sole reason that the seed of devotion is sown amid our deeds, the Lord's love elates our inner self on the threshold of desires, and then the take-off of our spiritual journey begins while being in the mortal coil. The Lord taps our basic self, lying dormant inside us, in an incarnated form that He had adorned for us, pushing us towards our true mission while we are bound to this body. He awakens us to attain the Lord, hence bathing us in the devotional Light of the Lord. He alone shows us the true light even amid the darkness of Maya.

O Mortal being, wake up to each knock of the Lord. To awaken your inner self, listen to His silent language and recognise His footsteps that make no sound. Make this silent language, light knock, the sound of His footsteps the aim of your life as He is telling us a lot through these gestures, actions, leelas, as though He is singing the tune of His name in a language that is showering His Divine grace on us, silently, quietly. Keep this divine melody of His name always on your lips. Imbibe it in your inner self in such a way that each pore of your body only sings His name and each breath radiates His name alone. This means that to attain Moksha or liberation, our body may be alive or it may perish but His name always remains, introducing us to the pious self, the unending, uninterrupted, unborn form of the Lord inside us, hence making us embrace liberation. This body is only a means to carry this soul to its origin, the supersoul and to show the right path to this mortal being, to remind it of its true aim of life, over and over again, The Lord Himself incarnates on this earth, as our Guru God. He gives us a glimpse of His ever-alive self with the power of His name, makes us walk on this amazing path that He walks with us, hence finally merging our identity in His own Divine identity. It's only at this point that He rests in peace with the mission achieved. He never lets His children go off track till they do not achieve their true identity, that is, merge into the Lord Almighty.

We have been assigned this mortal coil
made of five elements.
To fill life into this coil,
the Lord Himself places a speck of Himself (as soul).
Hence giving life to this coil
to be able to perform 'deeds'.
As we have got a form from the earth
hence we are lost in things created by the earth.
We keep living a normal (mortal) life,
but unfortunately forget the 'true form' of life,
hence dancing to the egoistic tune of this body.
This body is only a means to realise what is 'true life'.
The mortal coil is only a medium for us to merge into the unborn.

The five senses only control our five elements,

mind, intellect and ego.

Only the consorts of 'faith' and 'patience' lead us onto attaining victory over all offshoots of Maya,

all things born of Maya.

They (faith, patience) make us walk on the path paved by their master (Lord Almighty).

Making us hold the hand of the Lord,

to ultimately reach Him

hence, giving us deliverance by merging into 'Him'.

The Lord appears in an 'incarnated' form on this earth,

solely for 'Human Upliftment'

and on the completion of the 'Divine task'

the avtaar He adorns once again merges into their ever-alive, omnipresent form

always smiling for us in His 'ever-alive' form.

In every Yuga they (the incarnated form of the Lord) show, through the mortal coil

the true path to reach within.

They appear as an incarnation

at times is called 'Maryada Purushottam' (Rama),

hence wandering in the forests

at other times the Lord appears as a cowherd boy (Krishna)

to eat the butter of love and devotion,

yet at other times God appears as Datta Bhagwan

from the pious home of Ansuya Maa

to bathe this creation in 'bliss'.

To save His own offshoots (we beings)
from the horrendous pace, heat of destruction of this Kalyug.
He appears in new incarnations of the Datta Swarupa,
over and over again.
As Shri Narsimh Saraswati, Shi Pad Vallabh ji.
Shi Gajanan Maharaj, Shri Akkalkot Swami
and as Shri Sai Baba of Shirdi.
By Making this incarnated mortal coil a means,
holding our hand, beyond the bondages of the body,
above the five senses.
He introduces us to the soul within
playing on the strings of devotional love.
By the loving joy of His name
and by His Divine Touch.
He teaches, us Humans, what is 'true humanity'.
How we have to attain the Lord,
while in this 'mortal coil'.
He shows us over and over again with His leelas,
His mannerisms, His so called deeds.
He keeps repeating this till we start moving towards
our true aim (Liberation)...

For this the Lord takes a new form
He appears on this earth over and over again for us...
To shine with joy, only after ferrying us across this ocean of mundane existence...
To rest in peace, only after merging His own identity (soul) into the supersoul (Lord).

I was, I am, I always will be...

Incarnations come and go, appear and disappear bodily

But the Lord (the true form) is omnipresent,

He introduces, us mortal beings, to His 'unmanifest' form by 'Manifesting' in a form.

After which He once again merges in His omnipresent, unborn, ever-alive form, that is, realised in omnipresence.

At some places 'His Lotus feet' speak

and at other's 'His Samadhi' communicates.

But the reality, the fact remains

that each devotee is showered by His Divne grace

according to each one's capacity, capability and old ties of give and take,

devotion, love and above all 'The Lord's grace'.

This grace flows before an incarnation appears,

from the pious hands of the incarnated form

and after the mission of the incarnation is achieved

Always... forever...

Om Sai Ram!

Our Books on SHIRDI SAI BABA

Shirdi Sai Baba is a household name in India as well as in many parts of the World today. These books offer fascinating glimpses into the life and miracles of Shirdi Sai Baba and other Perfect Masters. These books will provide you with an experience that is bound to transform one's sense of perspective and bring about perceptible and meaningful spiritual growth.

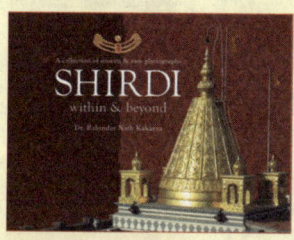

SHIRDI within & beyond
A collection of unseen & rare photographs
Dr. Rabinder Nath Kakarya
ISBN 978 81 207 7806 1
₹ 750

Baba's Divine Symphony
Vinny Chitluri
ISBN 978 81 207 8485 7
₹ 250

The Loving God: Story of Shirdi Sai Baba
Dr. G. R. Vijayakumar
ISBN 978 81 207 8079 8
₹ 200

The Age of Shirdi Sai Baba
Dr. C. B. Satpathy
ISBN 978 81 207 8700 1
₹ 225

Life History of Shirdi Sai Baba
Ammula Sambasiva Rao
ISBN 978 81 207 7722 4
₹ 150

The Eternal Sai Phenomenon
A R Nanda
ISBN 978 81 207 6086 8
₹ 200

Ek An English Musical on the Life of Shirdi Sai Baba
Usha Akella
ISBN 978 81 207 6842 0
₹ 75

SHRI SAI SATCHARITA
The Life and Teachings of Shirdi Sai Baba
Translated by Indira Kher
ISBN 978 81 207 2811 8 ₹ 500(HB)
ISBN 978 81 207 2153 1 ₹ 300(PB)

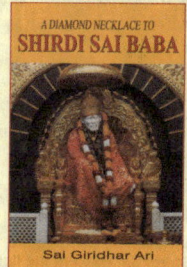

A Diamond Necklace To: Shirdi Sai BabaSai
Giridhar Ari
ISBN 978 81 207 5868 1
₹ 200

Shri Sai Baba's Teachings & Philosophy
Lt Col M B Nimbalkar
ISBN 978 81 207 2364 1
₹ 100

BABA- May I Answer
C.B. Satpathy
ISBN 978 81 207 4594 0
₹ 150

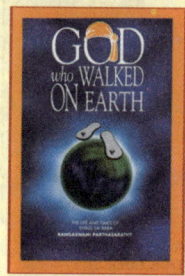

God Who Walked on Earth:
The Life & Times of Shirdi Sai Baba
Rangaswami Parthasarathy
ISBN 978 81 207 1809 8
₹ 150

STERLING

SHIRDI SAI BABA

Baba's Vaani: His Sayings and Teachings
Compiled by Vinny Chitluri
ISBN 978 81 207 3589 1
₹ 200

Baba's Gurukul SHIRDI
Vinny Chitluri
ISBN-978-81-207-4770-8
₹ 200

Baba's Anurag Love for His Devotees
Compiled by Vinny Chitluri
ISBN 978 81 207 5447 8
₹ 125

Baba's Rinanubandh Leelas during His Sojoum in Shir
Compiled by Vinny Chitluri
ISBN 978 81 207 3403 6
₹ 200

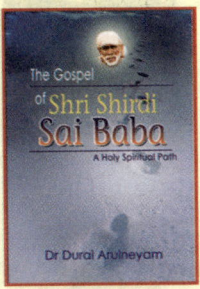

The Gospel of Shri Shirdi Sai Baba: A Holy Spiritual Path
Dr Durai Arulneyam
ISBN 978 81 207 3997 0
₹ 150

Sai Baba's 261 Leelas
Balkrishna Panday
ISBN 978 81 207 2727 4
₹ 125

Spotlight on the Sai Story
Chakor Ajgaonker
ISBN 978 81 207 4399 1
₹ 125

Shirdi Sai Baba A Practical God
K. K. Dixit
ISBN 978 81 207 5918 3
₹ 75

A Solemn Pledgefrom True Tales of Shirdi Sai Baba
Dr B H Briz-Kishore
ISBN 978 81 207 2240 8
₹ 95

I am always with you
Lorraine Walshe-Ryan
ISBN 978 81 207 3192 9
₹ 150

Shirdi Sai Baba
Vikas Kapoor
ISBN 987 81 207 59701
₹ 30

Unravelling the Enigma: Shirdi Sai Baba in the light of Sufism
Marianne Warren
ISBN 978 81 207 2147 0
₹ 400

STERLING

Sab Ka Malik Ek

**Shirdi Sai Baba
The Divine Healer**
Raj Chopra
ISBN 978 81 207 4766 1
₹ 100

**Shirdi Sai Baba and
other Perfect Masters**
C B Satpathy
ISBN 978 2384 15081 207 9
₹ 150

The Miracles of Sai Baba
ISBN 978 81 207 5433 1 (HB)
₹ 250

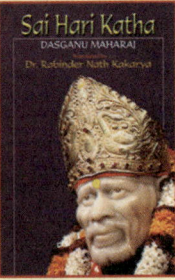

Sai Hari Katha
*Dasganu Maharaj Translated by
Dr. Rabinder Nath Kakarya*
ISBN 978 81 207 3324 4
₹ 100

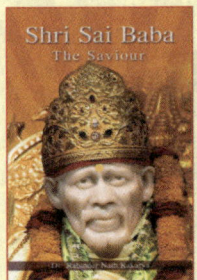

Shri Sai Baba- The Saviour
Dr. Rabinder Nath Kakarya
ISBN 978 81 207 4701 2
₹ 100

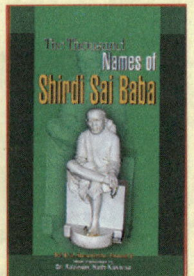

**The Thousand Names of
Shirdi Sai Baba**
*Sri B.V. Narasimha Swami Ji
Hindi translation by
Dr. Rabinder Nath Kakarya*
ISBN 978 81 207 3738 9
₹ 75

Sri Sai Baba
*Swami Sai Sharan Anand
Translated by V.B Kher*
ISBN 978 81 207 1950 7
₹ 200

**Sai Baba: His Divine
Glimpses**
V B Kher
ISBN 978 81 207 2291 0
₹ 95

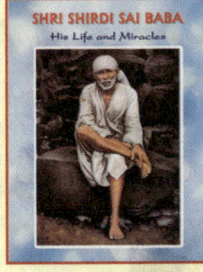

**Shri Shirdi Sai Baba: His
Life and Miracles**
ISBN 978 81 207 2877 6
₹ 25

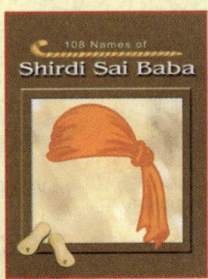

**108 Names of
Shirdi Sai Baba**
ISBN 978 81 207 3074 8
₹ 50

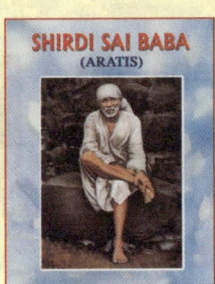

Shirdi Sai Baba Aratis
(English)   ₹ 10

**Shirdi Sai Speaks...
Sab Ka Malik Ek
Quotes for the Day**
ISBN 81 207 3101 200978 1
₹ 200

STERLING

SHIRDI SAI BABA

Divine Gurus

Hazrat Babajan:
A Pathan Sufi of Poona
Kevin R. D. Shepherd
ISBN 978 81 207 8698 1
₹ 200

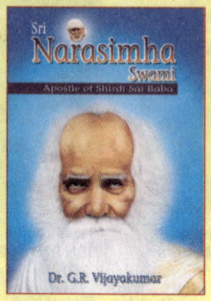

Sri Narasimha Swami
Apostle of Shirdi Sai Baba
Dr. G.R. Vijayakumar
ISBN 978 81 207 4432 5
₹ 90

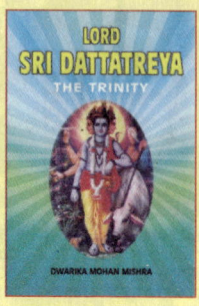

Lord Sri Dattatreya
The Trinity
Dwarika Mohan Mishra
ISBN 978 81 207 5417 1
₹ 200

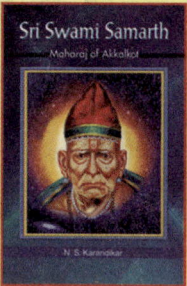

Sri Swami Samarth
Maharaj of Akkalkot
N.S. Karandikar
ISBN 978 81 207 3445 6
₹ 200

Guru Charitra
Shree Swami Samarth
ISBN 978 81 207 3348 0
₹ 200

Shirdi Sai Baba Box

Shri Sai Baba
978 81 207 6920 5
Box size: 23.5 x 16.5 cm
₹900

Shri Sai Satcharitra

Vibhuti

Dateless Calendar

Sai Baba Mandiramdhil
Arataya & Mantrochar - Mp3

Sai Baba Photo Frame

STERLING

श्री शिरडी साई बाबा

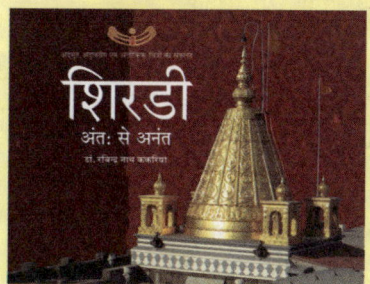  

शिरडी अंत: से अनंत
डॉ. रबिन्द्रनाथ ककरिया
978 81 207 8191 7
₹ 750

श्री साई सच्चरित्र
श्री शिरडी साई बाबा की अद्भुत जीवनी तथा उनके अमूल्य उपदेश
गोविंद रघुनाथ दाभोलकर (हेमाडपंत)
978 81 207 2501 0   ₹ 250 (PB)
978 81 207 2500 3   ₹ 300 (HB)

साई सुमिरन
अंजु टंडन
978 81 207 8706 3
₹ 90

बाबा की वाणी-उनके वचन तथा उपदेश
बेला शर्मा
978 81 207 4745 6
₹ 100

बाबा का अनुराग
विनी चितलुरी
978 81 207 6699 0
₹ 100

बाबा का ऋणानुबंध
विनी चितलुरी
978 81 207 5998 5
₹ 125

बाबा का गुरूकुल-शिरडी
विनी चितलुरी
978 81 207 6698 3
₹ 125

साई की आत्मकथा
विकास कपूर
978 81 207 7719 4
₹ 200

साई संवाद
उर्मिल सत्य भूषण
978 81 207 7777 4
₹ 200

बाबा-आध्यात्मिक विचार
चन्द्र भानुसतपथी
978 81 207 4627 5
₹ 150

साई शरण में
चन्दुभानु सतपथी
978 81 207 2802 8
₹ 150

श्री शिरडी साई बाबा

श्री शिरडी साई बाबा एवं अन्य सद्गुरु
चन्द्रभानु सतपथी
978 81 207 4401 1
₹ 90

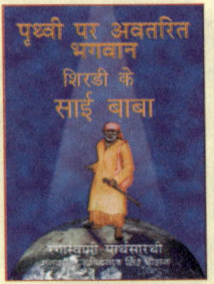

पृथ्वी पर अवतरित भगवान शिरडी के साई बाबा
रंगास्वामी पार्थसारथी
978 81 207 2101 2
₹ 150

साई - सबका मालिक
कल्पना भाकुनी
978 81 207 3320 6
₹ 125

साई बाबा एक अवतार
बेला शर्मा
978 81 207 6706 5
₹ 100

साई सत् चरित का प्रकाश
बेला शर्मा
978 81 207 7804 7
₹ 200

श्री साई बाबा के परम भक्त
डॉ. रबिन्द्रनाथ ककरिया
978 81 207 2779 3
₹ 75

श्री साई बाबा के उपदेश व तत्त्वज्ञान
लेफ्टिनेन्ट कर्नल एम. बी. निंबालकर
978 81 207 5971 8   ₹ 100

साई भक्तानुभव
डॉ. रबिन्द्रनाथ ककरिया
978 81 207 3052 6
₹ 90

श्री साई बाबा के अनन्य भक्त
डॉ. रबिन्द्र नाथ ककरिया
978 81 207 2705 2
₹ 75

साई का संदेश
डॉ. रबिन्द्र नाथ ककरिया
978 81 207 2879 0
₹ 125

शिरडी संपूर्ण दर्शन
डॉ. रबिन्द्रनाथ ककरिया
978 81 207 2312 2
₹ 50

मुक्ति दाता - श्री साई बाबा
डॉ. रबिन्द्रनाथ ककरिया
978 81 207 2778 6
₹ 65

सबका मालिक एक

श्री नरसिम्हा स्वामी
शिरडी साई बाबा के
दिव्य प्रचारक
डॉ. रबिन्द्र नाथ ककरिया
978 81 207 4437 0   ₹ 75

साई दत्तावधूता
राजेन्द्र भण्डारी
978 81 207 4400 4
₹ 75

साई हरि कथा
दासगणु महाराज
978 81 207 3323 7
₹ 65

शिरडी साई बाबा - की सत्य
कथाओं से प्राप्त - एक पावन
प्रतिज्ञा
प्रो. डॉ. बी.एच. ब्रिज-किशोर
978 81 207 2346 7   ₹ 80

शिरडी साई बाबा की दिव्य
लीलाएँ
डॉ. रबिन्द्र नाथ ककरिया
978 81 207 6376 0   ₹ 150

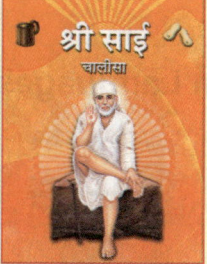

श्री साई चालीसा
ISBN 978 81 207 4773 9
₹ 50

शिरडी साई बाबा
विकास कपूर
978 81 207 5969 5
₹ 30

Shirdi Sai Baba Aratis
(Hindi)   ₹10

शिरडी साई के दिव्य वचन-सब का मालिक एक
प्रतिदिन का विचार
978 81 207 3533 0
₹ 180

श्री शिरडी साई बाबा

Oriya Language Books

श्री साई सच्चरित्र (Oriya)
श्री गोविन्दराव रघुनाथ दाभोळकर
(हेमाडपंत)
978 81 207 6332 4 ₹ 300

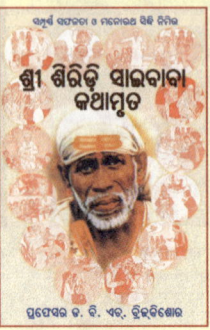
श्री शिरिडी साईबाबा कथामृत
प्रोफेसर ज. वि. एस. कृष्णकिशोर (Oriya)
978 81 207 7774 3
₹ 80

शिरिडी साई बाबांक जीवन चरित (Oriya)
अमूल शायरीव राव
अनुवादक – किशोर चन्द्र पट्टनायक
978 81 207 7417 9 ₹ 100

Other Indian Languages

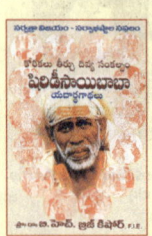
शिरडी साईबाबा (Telugu)
प्रो. डॉ. बी.एच. ब्रिज-किशोर
978 81 207 2294 1
₹ 80

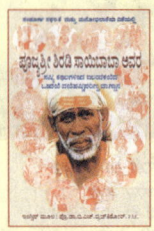
(Kannada)
प्रो. डॉ. बी.एच. ब्रिज-किशोर
978 81 207 2873 8
₹ 80

(Tamil)
प्रो. डॉ. बी.एच. ब्रिज-किशोर
978 81 207 2876 9
₹ 80

Shirdi Sai Baba Aratis
(Kannada) ₹10

Shirdi Sai Baba Aratis
(Tamil) ₹10

Shirdi Sai Baba Aratis
(Telugu) ₹10

शिरडी साई बाबा (भोजपुरी)
विकास कपूर
978 81 207 7558 9
₹ 30

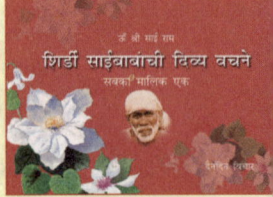
शिर्डी साईबाबांची दिव्य वचने (Marathi)
सबका मालिक एक
दैनंदिन विचार
978 81 207 7518 3 ₹ 180

STERLING PUBLISHERS PVT. LTD.
A-59, Okhla Industrial Area, Phase-II, New Delhi-110020,
For Online order & detailed Catalogue visit our website:
www.sterlingpublishers.com, E-mail : mail@sterlingpublishers.com, Tel. 91-11-26386165, 2638